The Mood of the Fifth

A Musical Approach to Early Childhood

EDITED BY NANCY FOSTER

The Mood of the Fifth: A Musical Approach to Early Childhood
First English Edition

ISBN: 978-1-936849-21-5

Editor: Nancy Foster
Copy Editor and Graphic Design: Lory Widmer
Cover Painting: Sheila Harrington

We gratefully acknowledge the publishers who granted permission to reprint the following material:

Wynstones Press (www.wynstonespress.com), for "The Value of Music in the Life of the Young Child" by Jennifer Aulie from the Wynstones Kindergarten Series

Hawthorn Press (www.hawthornpress.com) for "Musical Forces and the Mood of the Fifth," excerpted from *Under the Stars* by Renate Long-Breipohl; and for "Music for Young Children" by Rita Jacobs, excerpted from the book *Music for Young Children*

The Association for Healing Education for "The Erosion of Listening" by Sheila Phelps Johns

Steiner Waldorf Schools Fellowship, for "If music be the food of love, play on" by Sally Schweizer, "What Is the 'Right Thing' for the Child?" by Estelle Bryer, "The Creation of Tone" by Sarah Weber, and "Singing with Pre-school Children" by Michael Deason-Barrow, from *Kindling: The Journal for Steiner Waldorf Early Childhood Care and Education*

Acorn Hill Waldorf Kindergarten and Nursery, for "Musical Instruments in the Classroom?" from *In a Nutshell* by Nancy Foster

This publication was made possible by a grant from the Waldorf Curriculum Fund.

Waldorf Early Childhood Association of North America
285 Hungry Hollow Rd.
Spring Valley, NY 10977
845-352-1690
info@waldorfearlychildhood.org
www.waldorfearlychildhood.org

For a complete book catalog, contact WECAN or visit our online store:
store.waldorfearlychildhood.org

THE MOOD OF THE FIFTH

Contents

The World of Tone: Singing, Sounding, Listening

Note

The notes of the scale beginning with middle C are indicated within the text as c′, d′, e′, f′, g′, a′, b′, c″ (with the double mark indicating the beginning of the second octave), and so on.

The pentatonic scale starting on the D above middle C is indicated as d′, e′, g′, a′, b′, d″, e″.

Foreword

NANCY BLANNING

The moment which called this book into existence occurred in the Great Hall of the Goetheanum in Dornach, Switzerland, during the 2012 International Waldorf Early Childhood Conference. Dr. Renate Long-Breipohl, early childhood educator, researcher, lecturer, and teacher trainer, made the following remark in her keynote address:

> *Music is an integral part of our work in early childhood, and is especially healing when we surround the children with the lightness and gentleness of sound in the mood of the fifth. The experience of music in the mood of the fifth, its liveliness and openness towards the periphery, can become a vehicle for the "I" and the astral body in pervading and enlivening the whole child. Here are tremendous tasks for the early childhood educator, because up to this day the mood of the fifth is not given the chance to play the therapeutic role it could have for young children.*

The dictionary gives two definitions for "therapeutic:" 1) serving to cure or heal; 2) serving to preserve health. While we know that little children are just getting started in life and are striving toward perfection in their development, we also see that the world around them is not very supportive to this end. We see children with delays and discontinuous development from mild to severe. These children are not ill, but they do have a need for therapeutic support of healthy growth in body, soul, and spirit.

As teachers we need to employ all possibilities to encourage the children's healthy incarnation. Few of us have had the chance to deepen our background in therapeutic approaches. *But we all sing, every day.* Dr. Long-Breipohl's comment suggests that we have not begun to fathom the potential for how healing and encouraging mood-of-the-fifth music can be for our little children. If we can deepen our understanding of this music, cultivate it within our own souls, and practice it every day, this potentized song can reach every child in every class as a healing balm. Even healthy children need this in our increasingly frantic and sometimes assaulting world.

My own music education is very limited. Everything I know about the mood of the fifth I have learned from Nancy Foster. So when this idea began to itch and she was asked to bring this book forward, she was gracious enough to agree. Thank you, Nancy. And thank you to each of the authors who have contributed their own experience and research. The benefits for teaching colleagues and children are going to be huge.

Introduction

NANCY FOSTER

To create an environment that nourishes the young children in our care. . . an environment filled with beauty, warmth, and joy. . . an environment that supports the child's growth in body, soul, and spirit: This is our goal as adults inspired by Waldorf education. And music is part of that environment!

Rudolf Steiner tells us that "song is an earthly means of recalling the experience of pre-earthly existence."[1] How can we joyfully do honor to this inspiring thought?

Long ago, as a new teacher, I was very pleased to have learned a few chords on the guitar to accompany favorite songs with the children. Then I attended my first Waldorf conference which included a session with a venerated pioneer of music in Waldorf early childhood education. Very sternly she admonished us, "*Never* play guitar with the children!" Fortunately I was able to take this as an interesting challenge rather than a devastating blow—and thus began my journey into an approach to music that was new to me.

This journey received a further impetus some years later when I attended another workshop and was introduced to mood-of-the-fifth music. I had grown up in a family of musicians and had played cello since early childhood, so I was completely attuned to classical music. To me, this mood-of-the-fifth music sounded very strange. I recall thinking to myself, "Well, this music is *odd* and I'm just not going to use it." And that was that . . . or so I thought.

As it turned out, however, in the 1980s Elisabeth Moore-Haas, from the teacher training seminar in Bern, Switzerland, came to our school to offer a three-week course on "The Musical Approach to Early Childhood." Here I learned much more about mood-of-the-fifth music, and why it was important for young children in the context of human and cosmic evolution. This was the missing piece for me: the *why* of this music. I realized that in music—as in other aspects of our work with young children—it is our responsibility to reach beyond our comfort zone for the sake of the children, and to strive selflessly to offer what is most health-giving for them.

And so I set out to become comfortable with this new kind of music. I began to be an "experimenter." The first year, I chose one mood-of-the-fifth song that we would sing every day, at the beginning of circle time. Gradually I added more mood-of-the-fifth songs, until the "musical framework" of the morning—the songs we sang every day at the same times—were in the mood of the fifth, as well as many of the songs in our seasonal circles. This began to feel as natural and comfortable as could be. In fact, it felt *right*.

After many years of experimenting with the mood of the fifth, I am so glad to be able to offer this collection of articles by our colleagues in the Waldorf movement! Many teachers find the journey into mood-of-the-fifth music a bit daunting; and many may share my resistance to making such a journey just because "we are supposed to." The authors in our collection present a wide variety of approaches to this topic, sharing their own experiences and research into the "what, why, and how" of mood-of-the-fifth music.

We have divided the book into three sections. The first section, ***First Steps into the Mood of the Fifth***, offers an introductory look at the mood of the fifth, to give a feel for what this is all about, without a great deal of technical detail.

The articles in the second section, ***Deeper Insights into the Mood of the Fifth***, delve more deeply into mood-of-the-fifth music, exploring its history and its place in human and cosmic evolution, and in some cases offering a detailed presentation of music history and theory. (The glossary of musical terms offered in the Rita Jacobs article in the first section may be of help here.)

The third section, ***The World of Tone: Singing, Sounding, Listening***, broadens the perspective beyond specifically mood-of-the-fifth music to the wider realm of tone itself—approaches to singing, to instrumental music, and to *listening*, so essential to consider in our world today.

There is no doubt that music in the mood of the fifth requires serious thought and practice. *But*—as Sally Schweizer's article reminds us, music is a source of joy in human life! If, in our efforts to do the "right" thing, we lose this joy, are we really serving the children's best interests? Rudolf Steiner reminds us that the children "need teachers that look and act with happiness and, most of all, with honest unaffected love. Such a love that streams, as it were, with warmth through the physical environment of the children may be said to literally 'hatch' the forms of the physical organs."[2]

As a student of anthroposophy, I have always appreciated Rudolf Steiner's many warnings against dogmatism and one-sidedness, and he tells us that the teacher must never become stale, but rather "cherish a mood of soul which is fresh and healthy."[3] For me, taking up mood-of-the-fifth music was certainly a matter of serious intention; but then, it was essential to transform this seriousness into the joy of singing with the children. I discovered that for me, mood of the fifth can apply to the mood of the whole experience of the early childhood morning or day, and that when this mood pervades the whole, other music, such as simple folk melodies and the rich tradition of singing games, can be brought and embraced within this whole. Each of us can find our way with this.

And so, with heartfelt thanks to all who have made this book possible, I wish you the very best, and much joy, in your own journey with mood-of-the-fifth music.

Notes

1. Rudolf Steiner, *The Inner Nature of Music and the Experience of Tone*, Lecture 4, Dornach, December 2, 1922 (Anthroposophic Press), p. 35. This lecture cycle contains important statements that are frequently (and sometimes repeatedly) cited in the following chapters, as each author strives to understand Steiner's insights in his or her own way. It is a fundamental source for our work on this topic.

2. Rudolf Steiner. "The Education of the Child in the Light of Spiritual Science," in *The Education of the Child and Early Lectures on Education* (Great Barrington, MA: Anthroposophic Press, 1996), p. 22.

3. Rudolf Steiner. *Practical Advice to Teachers* (London: Rudolf Steiner Press, 1976), p. 200.

PART ONE

First Steps into the Mood of the Fifth

The Value of Music in the Life of the Young Child

JENNIFER FLOYD AULIE

This article originally appeared in the series of seasonal books from Wynstones Press, Spring, Summer, Autumn, Winter, Gateways, *and* Spindrift *(third edition, 1999) and is included here with the kind permission of the author and publisher. Here we are introduced to the realm of the early childhood classroom and to the musical mood that can surround the children in a living, healing way.*

Free Play in a Waldorf Kindergarten

It is a winter morning: the twenty children are busy with their work. The youngest, three- and four-year-olds, are helping the teacher chop apples for snack; some five-year-old girls are taking care of their "children" in the doll corner; next to them is a group of five-year-old boys and girls who are sitting at a round table polishing stones, grating chestnuts and chatting together. In the center of the room, an observant and energetic four-year-old boy is directing the six-year-olds in the construction of a snowplow: tables are stacked on each other, chairs turned upside down and leaned against the tables for the front part of the plow. A large basket of chestnuts is balanced on top of the plow. The chestnuts are grit and salt, to be scattered later on the plowed streets. The room is small and the noise level is moderately high.

Underneath the windows, on the carpet where the children have a free space to build up scenes and play with standing puppets and animals, a six-year-old girl sits, absorbed in her work. She has laid out a forest of pinecones, which stands on the banks of a river of blue cloth. Stepping stones allow the poor shepherd boy, who lives at the edge of the forest, to cross the river and wind his way to the castle gates nearby. The princess, leaning out of her tower, sees him coming and calls down to him. . .

As she lays out the scene, the girl accompanies her actions with narrative, speaking in a soft tone, sometimes almost whispering to herself. When the puppets begin to live in the scene her voice changes, becoming more sung than spoken, the pitch of her spoken voice being taken over by her singing voice. Her recitative is not sing-song rhythmic, but the rhythm freely moves with the intention of the shepherd boy as he jumps from stone to stone. The pitch of the girl's voice is a colorful monotone: the pitch remains much the same, but the tone color is enlivened through the intensity and quality of the words as the shepherd crosses the stream. There are moments when a word is spoken, then the narrative is sung again.

When the shepherd arrives at the castle gates, the princess calls down to him from her high tower. She is faraway, and the girl reaches up with her voice to the distant place where the princess lives, and sings her greetings down to the shepherd. The girl's voice is high now, but the intervals she sings are not large, they are between a third and a fifth. The high pitch of her voice, although it is not loud, has attracted some of the five-year-olds: several come over to the rug and lie on their stomachs, watching the play unfold. The shepherd now tells the princess of his wish that she come down and go with him. The simple recitative changes to a declamatory aria: a melody of several different tones arises, moving stepwise, the girl's voice becomes more intense as the shepherd pleads his cause. There is little repetition in the melody, but the movement contained in it provides a musical mood which waits expectantly for the princess's reply . . .

In the meantime, the snowplow has already cleared quite a few streets. It has come back to make a second round to scatter the grit and salt . . . The four-year-olds slicing apples jump up from the table. The noise of all those chestnuts hitting a wooden floor is so wonderful, they want to join the fun! The "mothers" putting their children to bed are angry that the snowplow has woken up their little ones, now the babies are crying . . . Some of the children polishing stones and grating chestnuts try throwing their stones and chestnuts on the floor—what a good idea, it makes a lovely *cracking* sound . . .

. . . The five-year-olds listening to the play hold their breaths as the princess agrees to go with the shepherd but he must first ask permission from her father, the king . . . The princess's instructions are sung to him in a melody of seconds with a strong, definite rhythm . . .

An observer can hardly believe that the chestnut-strewn chaos in the other half of the room (which the teacher is quickly helping to put right again) does not seem to penetrate the sheath of peacefulness which surrounds the puppet play. The children gathered around it show no sign that anything else in the room has taken place . . . At the successful conclusion of the play, the children watching it lie still. The girl covers the scene with a cloth and sings in a half-whispering tone a farewell to the story of the shepherd and the princess. As her voice fades, there is a moment of absolute silence. Then the five-year-olds run back to the polishing table and the girl goes to the teacher to ask how long it will be until snack.

This description of a six-year-old girl's singing contains many elements of what has come to be called music in the "mood of the fifth": the singing follows the rhythm of speech; melodies are simple, moving within intervals of seconds and thirds, sometimes as large as a fifth, rarely larger; melodies are often sung on one tone, the pitch taken from the speaking voice; the melodies are not written in major or in minor keys and have an open-ended feel to them. Above all is the mood of the music: when sung properly it seems to reach out and enfold the children in a protective sheath which has a quality of stillness and peace, although the children themselves may be active within it.

This music is a musical expression of an experience which is striven for in all aspects of Waldorf education. It is difficult to describe in words, perhaps: "I am centered in my activity," "My thinking, feeling and willing are in balance." One feels deeply united with a task, at peace and yet still active. The young child finds this mood in play. She is deeply engaged in an activity which is then no longer interesting when the activity is over. The moment of silence at the end of the play was not a moment of reflection, but a moment which allowed the activity of watching the play to come to a complete end before the next task could engage the children's attention.

The broader context of this musical experience should be noted: the kindergarten just described is one where mood-of-the-fifth music was not cultivated by the teacher. The children learned only traditional children's songs and games which were sung in strict rhythm, and with major or minor key melodies. The six-year-old girl experienced similar music at home.

Yet the girl's singing is not an isolated or unusual musical event. Such singing can often be heard when a child's attention is fully engaged in play. We grown-ups tend to dismiss such fragments of melody as noise, or incomplete attempts by the child to sing our music, not listening closely enough to discover the innate coherence of the child's activity. Too often, well-meaning adults try to "correct" the pitch which is too high, or the rhythm which is irregular, and slowly wall in a living musicality with "proper" songs . . . Sooner or later, often at puberty, an attempt is made at breaking through these walls, as the pounding beat of popular music has long suggested.

The use of mood-of-the-fifth music in the kindergarten encompasses two considerations. It is, first of all, a path of musical development for the adult, which schools her musical perception and ability so that she is able to participate in a musicality which the children already possess. This musicality may, for many reasons, lie dormant or misshapen within an individual child or group of children. Through the adult's use of the mood of the fifth she can reawaken and bring back into movement the musicality which is so essential for the full development of the child's soul life. (To be labeled "unmusical" or "tone deaf" causes deep, lingering wounds to the child's self esteem. There are unfortunately many adults who can attest to the truth of this statement out of their own experience.)

Mood-of-the-fifth music can also help the adult to establish an additional point of contact with the child which shows him that the adult understands. One of the rewards of working with young children is surely the open look of delight on a child's face when he hears a story, plays a game, experiences something which pleases him. The look of delight means more, however, than just "I like that." On a deeper level it expresses the child's trust in the adult: "You know who I am, and what you offer me is that which I am searching for with my deepest intentions. I can follow you."

The present-day task of the Waldorf kindergarten is primarily a therapeutic one. It provides children with basic experiences which they need for healthy development, overcoming deficiencies which often occur today in the first years of life. A very large part of these experiences are sensory, as the development of the physical senses (touch, balance, etc.) lays the foundation for the later unfolding of the spiritual capacities (thinking, speech, etc). The kindergarten is not a mirror of our daily lives, but an extract of the many activities, distilled to their essence. This provides a simplicity and basic necessity for the content of kindergarten life which the child can understand and imitate wholeheartedly. The meaningful activity around the child awakens her interest in the world, and this interest becomes the mainspring of later learning.

In the arts, the materials presented to the child are restricted to essentials, and with these the child's imagination has free rein. This can be clearly seen, for example, in painting: the three primary colors are used—red, yellow and blue. The children are given watercolors, a large wet sheet of paper, and a broad brush to paint with. The materials themselves preclude any precise drawing, colors flow into one another, sometimes mixing, sometimes remaining pure side by side. There is no right or wrong way of using the colors, the expansive, fiery or cool moods of the colors themselves guide the child's brush. The medium of water enables the child's soul to breathe freely in the movement of color with the brush. If only the paper were bigger he could paint on and on . . .

Music can be approached in a similar way. Here as well the materials can be restricted so that the activity becomes of foremost importance. Only five different tones of our twelve tone system are used:

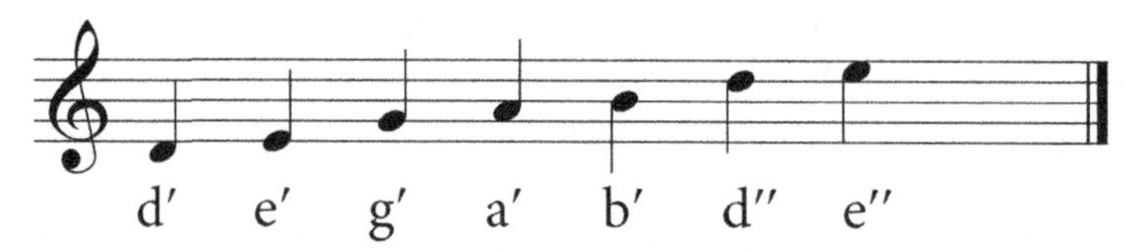

When a children's harp or lyre is used, the strings are tuned to pure fifths (like a violin's open strings) rather than the tempered intervals of the piano. The songs are not written in major or minor keys, but tend to circle around the middle tone, a′. The rhythm is free, either gently swinging (3 or 6 beats) or walking (2 or 4 beats), but the movement of the music takes its impulse from the words and seeks to accompany its inner content.

This style of music-making lends itself wonderfully to the activities of circle time where movement, the spoken word, and song freely flow from one to the other, just as the three basic colors do in painting. Teachers who have worked with mood-of-the-fifth music in the classroom also know of its effectiveness in creating moments where the attention of all of the children is engaged, enabling a special mood to arise, whether in a puppet play, grace before meal, etc.

Newcomers to this music may at first experience difficulty in hearing the melodies or finding an inner connection to them. Others may have trouble finding the beginning pitch or singing the songs as high as they are written. None of these difficulties should be considered unsolvable problems.

Over time, the practice of songs in the mood of the fifth often leads to a good sense of pitch. The voice gradually learns the placement of the tones, and the reduced number of tones make sight-singing possible even for the "unmusical" person.

Difficulty in reaching the higher notes (d″, e″), which lie within the traditional singing range of sopranos and altos, can be due to breathing which is too shallow, as well as to the false idea that high notes are more difficult to sing and require greater effort. In the long run, the question of extending the vocal range is best addressed by an experienced teacher. But those without a teacher can still consider the following: the vocal range can be affected by physical movement. Often much can be accomplished by accompanying a song with large, simple, physical gestures. This helps free the breathing, allowing greater ease in reaching notes which are "too high." The songs can be practiced with movement until the feeling of vocal mobility is secure. Then the outward movement can gradually become smaller and disappear altogether, all the while maintaining the inner freedom of movement in the voice.

An essential guide for adults who wish to find a path into the experience of mood-of-the-fifth music can be found in Julius Knierim's *Quintenlieder: Music for Young Children in the Mood of the Fifth*[1]. This succinct and clearly written booklet describes, with simple exercises and musical examples, a path which really can be taken by all who have a sincere interest in further development of their musical abilities. By working with the suggestions contained in Julius Knierim's essay, the serious student can develop capacities which not only lead one into the musical world of the young child, but can help build a new relationship to traditional classical music, and to all further musical development.

Rudolf Steiner, in discussing music for the young child, spoke of the great importance of the *Quintenstimmung* (Mood of the Fifth). The suggestions mentioned in this article, and most especially in Dr. Knierim's book, are guideposts by which adults may find the way into this mood. They are not the mood itself. Individual observation, experimentation, and practice are the means by which the letter of the law may be enlivened by its spirit.

Note

1. Dr. Julius Knierim, *Quintenlieder: Music for Young Children in the Mood of the Fifth* (Fair Oaks, CA: Rudolf Steiner College Press, 1994).

Jennifer Floyd Aulie was born and grew up in Michigan. She spent many summers on the eastern shore of Lake Michigan, where her family would gather in the evening to sing to the setting sun. She has lived in Europe for the past twenty years, working as a music teacher and music therapist. She really appreciates the work of Anthroposophical Prison Outreach.

Finding the Tonal Doorway to Early Childhood

The Mystery of Moods of Fifths

ELEANOR WINSHIP

In this article, we are guided into experiencing "the mystery of moods of fifths." Eleanor offers us the possibility of exploring the depths of Rudolf Steiner's insights into music and its relationship to the human being.

In a lecture about music in Stuttgart on March 7, 1923, Rudolf Steiner discussed the place of the interval of the fifth and other intervals in the evolution of humanity. He then spoke briefly of how up to the ninth year, the child lives essentially in moods of fifths (*Quintenstimmungen*) and should be approached with that understanding.[1] For years I, along with many others, have been pondering and exploring what sort of sound experiences he could have meant by "moods of fifths."

The mystery of moods of fifths deepens the more I experience just how wonderfully the music developed by the fine German musician Julius Knierim out of Steiner's brief indications can serve as a tonal doorway to the consciousness of early childhood. Knierim called his approach "mood of the fifth," rather than "moods of fifths." I still remember the look on my own children's faces when we visited a kindergarten years ago and the teacher was singing mood-of-the-fifth songs with her class. The class mood was hushed, eyes were wide open, and my children and I were captivated.

Mood-of-the-fifth songs touch upon the pulse of early childhood. They are subtle and flowing— similar to the rhythms of nature. This is not the clickety-clack, regular, and mechanical rhythm of a train on a track, a rhythm not to be found in nature. Knierim-inspired mood-of-the-fifth music tends to be unmetered and wafts like a breeze rustling the fall leaves or the snow gently floating down to earth. Or if the music is metered, its meter is fluid and changeable. Mood-of-the-fifth music can stay floating in the realm of early childhood—still intuitively connected to the cosmos and nature.

These flowing rhythms surround the child with a sense of well-being; you can feel this process of envelopment when you try mood of the fifth songs with children. One senses an almost palpable quiet out-breath in the children—a relaxed and peaceful attunement. There is nothing forced or artificial about the quality in the music that is engendering this process. These songs are not sentimental, and they need to be sung in an objectively quiet and peaceful way.

To reach this objective sense of quiet and peacefulness, the melodies need (and want!) to be sung with a pure and gentle tone, the less vibrato the better. Best is to sing clearly and simply on your breath stream, not pushing the tone. When the voice is not being pushed, the sound will gently surround the child, rather than rush past her, thereby creating a dome of tone. The melodies are tuned to the tone a′, and it might be helpful to have an instrument such as a children's harp or flute or tone bar to ring the a′ and then hum it before you begin.

What tones can help us create a foundation for the mood of the fifth? Consider the pattern of notes below (the pattern is drawn from Steiner's earlier remarks in the same lecture about the interval of the fifth). Although these notes form a pentatonic scale, it is best not to think of the pattern as a scale in the conventional sense.

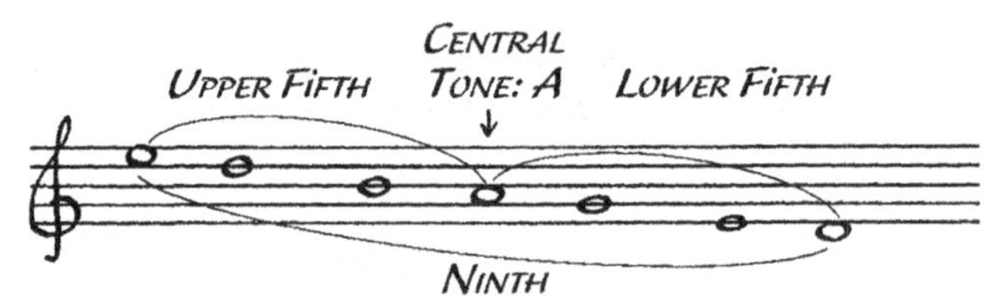

There are no half steps in this pattern. Using these tones without the smaller half steps and remaining centered on a′ is a good foundation to keep us hovering and away from major or minor inclinations. From a′, we can move up the space of a fifth to e″ through the notes of b′ and d″. Downward from a′, those tones are mirrored through another space of a fifth to d′, through the notes of g′ and e′. Mood-of-the-fifth songs don't end with a sense of having come firmly home to the earth on the tonic, unlike music in a mood of major or minor.

How do you find an experiential entrance into the mood of the fifth with these tones? I recommend taking a few moments of peace and quiet, perhaps early in the morning or at sunset (I turn off lights and sit on my bed or near the window) and take an instrument: harp or flute (whatever you play) and simply play the fifth interval using the notes a′ and d′ and a′ a few times. Let the tones ring. Then play the other fifth interval with the notes a′ and e″ and a′ several times. Dream into the sounds and feel the mood these tones create. Then using a′ as your central tone, play up and down a bit while surrounding the a′ with the other tones described above, always returning to a′. It may take a while to feel your way into these new—but ancient—moods of fifths. This is the opening into the child's musical language—a world still attuned to the flow of the natural world. It takes a quiet, meditative approach to begin to enter the mystery of the child's world. Mood-of-the-fifth songs, in their quiet and subtle way, open a door into this world.

Julius Knierim once explained to me that a main purpose of the many songs with open fifths in his influential book *Quintenlieder*[2]—songs emphasizing leaps between a′ and d′ and a′ and e″—was to teach people to get away from major and minor and into the right mood. However, he did not intend their emphasis on the open fifth pattern to be the only way to shape mood of the fifth melodies. It would be good if we were watchful not to get excessively attached to that pattern ourselves. Mood-of-the-fifth songs, as Knierim told me, should always have a natural melodic flow. As Steiner cautioned, it is important never to be pedantic or dogmatic.

One reason it is important not to be dogmatic is because we can't know today with precision what Steiner meant in his single reference to "moods of fifths." The mood-of-the-fifth melodic forms that Knierim unveiled are wonderfully, mysteriously appropriate for young children, and they serve as a unique aid for adults trying to get beneath the accumulated layers of their own musical experiences in order to understand and live into the musical consciousness of small children. Still, there is no reason to believe that they exhaust Steiner's indications about moods of fifths. In the same passage, Steiner said that as a "preparation" for later capacities, children could be exposed to major and minor moods, although they did not live in them yet. It is not surprising that anthroposophical musicians working with young children in the 1920s used a variety of approaches.[3] Steiner's "moods of fifths" are still a mystery inviting much further work, discussion, and exploration.

The above is only the briefest of introductions to moods of fifths. Explore for yourself the various ways people have sought to give expression to moods of fifths in this book and elsewhere, and for much, much more depth, study and contemplate Steiner's musical insights in *The Inner Nature of Music and the Experience of Tone*, where the Stuttgart lecture can be found. We are all beginners!

Notes

1. Rudolf Steiner, *The Inner Nature of Music and the Experience of Tone* (Spring Valley, NY: Anthroposophic Press, 1983), pp. 57-8.

2. Julius Knierim, *Quintenlieder: Music for Young Children in the Mood of the Fifth*, (Fair Oaks, CA: Rudolf Steiner College Press, 1994).

3. Gerhard Beilharz, "Julius Knierims Beitrag zur Musik für jüngere Kinder, mit einem Blick auf sein vor 33. Jahren erschienenes Quintenlieder-Heft," accessed at http://freie-musik-schule.de/sites/default/files/Julius%20Knierims%20Beitrag%20zur%20Musik%20f%C3%BCr%20j%C3%BCngere%20Kinder.pdf

Eleanor Winship, a longstanding K-12 Waldorf music teacher, is a graduate of the Waldorf School of Garden City, Juilliard Preparatory Division, and Oberlin Conservatory, where she studied violin, voice, conducting, and music pedagogy. Eleanor was trained extensively in Werbeck singing by Werbeck's pupil, Jürgen Schriefer (Werbeck was a Swedish opera singer who worked with Rudolf Steiner) and studied anthroposophical singing therapy with Thomas Adam. She has given numerous music workshops and courses at anthroposophical and Waldorf conferences, colleges, and training centers across several continents, besides mentoring and evaluating Waldorf school music programs.

Creating a Protective Tonal Space

WILMA ELLERSIEK

In these excerpts from Giving Love—Bringing Joy, *translated by Lyn and Kundry Willwerth and published by WECAN in 2005, the author offers a beautiful picture of the incarnation of the child as it can be embraced and supported through music.*

Rocking

At the Loom of Time
When a mother her baby is rocking,
See through the window the moon shining clear—
And when heaven the earth is loving,
That's when a mother rocks her baby dear.
—Gottfried Wolters

At birth, the child enters the space where gravity holds sway, and we are called upon again and again to offer for his or her well-being on the hard road to earth existence, the feeling of weightlessness. An especially good and effective means for this is rocking. To be rocked is, in some degree, a continuation of the feeling of rocking and being carried that the child experienced while yet unborn in the mother's womb as she walked the earth.

Moreover, we need to remember that the child, surrounded and carried before birth in the watery element within the womb, feels afterwards surrounded by air—the new element that carries tone and sound to the ear, indeed to the whole body structure.

Sounds, muffled to perception within the womb, are replaced by the experience of clear tones. Familiar sounds from the womb are reborn on a new level in the mother's singing. Thus rocking and singing belong together. There is nothing that small children, and also bigger ones, are so fond of as being rocked while being hummed or sung to. They prosper as though fed an especially nutritious food—a heavenly food.

Rocking, with the sound of voice and speech, is like a delicious nourishment. It is the bread and water of life that we bring the children. Through the mother's voice the child is united with the world. Just as before birth the Child was united with the mother by the umbilical cord, so after birth it is in large measure the mother's voice, so to speak a voice cord, that now unites the child with the mother, and through her with living on earth, where he wants to develop.

This bond is established in an especially intimate and profound way when the mother sings as she rocks. This is evidenced through countless lullabies. Every era has recognized the child's need for rocking. Cradles and rocking chairs were built and hammocks strung, yet nothing is so well-suited, so protective and enfolding as mother's lap or father's arm. The warmth of bodily contact is of great significance. Above all it is the place where the child lies at the mother's heart, hearing her heartbeat not only with his ear, but with his entire organism. Just as in the uterus before birth, after birth the child feels most protected in his mother's lap. (The noted author of children's books, Jakob Streit, tells that in Switzerland the common expression describing a harmonious, well-balanced person is that as a child he was "well-rocked.")

To have a newborn swim in water in order to give the feeling of weightlessness, as in the amniotic fluid, or to play tapes to the child of the sounds of circulation and heartbeat heard within the mother's body, is not what the child needs after he is born. Even though the child may be calmed by such an appeal to its prenatal memories, we need to be aware that this is a return to a part of life already overcome, already outgrown. A new approach needs to be found and given for the present and future form of being in order to fit the new bodily expectations. Electronic media doesn't meet this need. In order to satisfy the child's bodily needs, it is important throughout the first seven years, but especially in the first three years, to make possible the healthy formation of the body as the basis for the development of soul and mind.

On mother's lap, the child rests on his mother's heart. In the lullabies he feels the heartbeat on a higher level through well-formed speech and poetic rhythm. The constant repetition of similarities in the stress of speech and the experience of pulsation in song evokes a feeling of security within the child. Through rhyme, trust is strengthened. When at the end of two lines two syllables harmonize in the same sound, this fact is experienced throughout the whole body. It is like the fulfillment of a joyful expectation, for one can count on its recurring every time. This develops confidence. Literal meaning doesn't matter; it is the harmony or sound in its balancing effect that counts. To meet artistically formed speech in lullabies is to know security on a higher level. Speech is spiritual reality. In meeting it the child feels the presence of lap and enveloping protection, a home, as it were, transformed into a higher being.

A child is a person who needs to and wants to grow up; he needs a protected space in which to develop while being shielded from the adult world. This is especially true regarding the music the child hears. At birth, the harmony of the spheres had to be left behind, yet the music of the planets still resounds within. A reflection can be found here on earth in music created by human beings. The child under the age of seven can experience only a small part of the full range of the twelve-tone series of intervals of the fifth. This smaller range is called the "mood of the fifth" with central tone A. The child can be active within this "tonal space" in a beneficial way, as in it he still lives closely connected with the cosmos. By way of this tonal space a "safe enclosure" is formed wherein the child can rest as in the lap of the stars. It is an unclouded, emotion-free space of security, lifted out of all earthly unrest, comparable to our experience when, gazing at ancient icons with their gold background, we may feel ourselves embraced by the warm glow as in a veil of light that surrounds and protects us. It is important to consider all this when composing the melodies for lullabies.

When one becomes fully aware of how very much the child is exposed to conventional contemporary music, one should feel called upon to provide as often and as much as possible a different kind of tonal space, a sort of "protected realm," for the beginning of life's sojourn on earth.

Whoever wants to know the full blossom and wholesome fruit cannot get around providing for the plant a healthy, strengthening soil for it to take root and grow. For that reason, what is here presented [in the book *Giving Love—Bringing Joy*] is intended to be a "model" of lullabies for voice as well as for instruments such as those provided by Choroi, tuned in fifths with Central tone A. These songs have proven themselves over decades at home, in kindergartens and orphanages, as well as in workshops with mother and child groups in rhythmic-musically formed garne-units. The rest periods embedded in the games were felt to have profound healing qualities. It is hoped that both the songs and the use of elementary Choroi instruments will stimulate parents, teachers, curative educators, and others in the healing professions to choose and try out whatever fits their own situations, at the same time encouraging them to create their own melodies and texts in the same sense as those presented here.

The Experience of Rhythm in the First Seven Years

The feeling of rhythm in the first seven years of childhood is fundamental, based on pulsation. Pulsation is the initial element, the germinal cell of all rhythmic activity. It is the constant repetition of what is similar, yet not identical. Pulsation is the basic beat, oriented to the heartbeat, dividing the stream of time.

Pulsation has two aspects: it is the polarity between stress and relief, impulse and relaxation (usually denoted as "pause" or "rest"), in which something decisive occurs, namely the preparation for another impulse. The heartbeat also has two parts: a polarity of expansion and contraction (systole and diastole); in the same way, breathing has its polarity of exhalation and inhalation. Like pulse and breathing, pulsation is variable in tempo; like these it has an elastic ability to adjust and can become slower or faster, thus working as an enlivening element in time's flow. Pulsation forms the basis for all ordering of time.

In spite of the action of its movement, there is nothing merely mechanical about pulsation. It has nothing to do with the usual time counting music teachers use to accustom their pupils to a regular tempo, often with the well-known mechanical metronome as its basis. This mechanical metrical tempo measurement is a linear, non-living rate per second in which the "beat" is hammered out, partitioning, but carrying no forward movement such as one finds in the stress of pulsation. Through the metrical time-measure, all living streaming and breathing is destroyed. It has a deadly effect on all musical execution.

The precision of pulsation is different from that of the machine. It responds not to mechanical laws, but to those of life. Therefore it is not fixed, or monotonous; it is elastic in its constant alternation between phases of stress and relief.

Graphically illustrated:

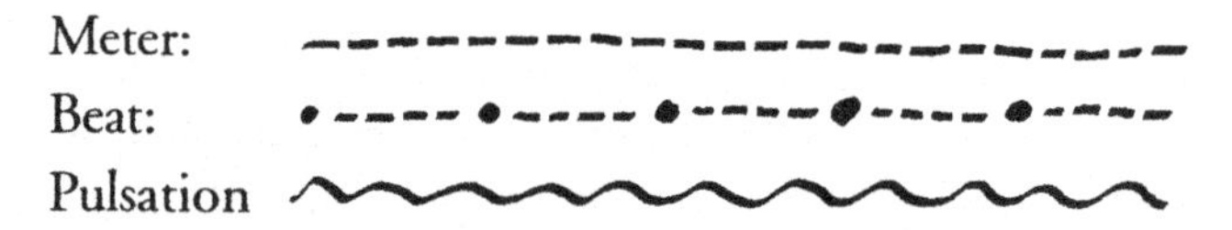

In the first seven years of life, the blood circulation and breathing only gradually become coordinated. A rhythmic relationship only slowly becomes established and stable. (This process actually only comes to its final equilibrium around the ninth year of life.) For this reason, one should spare children in this stage of life the rule of measure, beat, and fixed note value, for these are a harmful, disturbing, even destructive interference for the child.

Movement, speech and song should be brought to the child as pulsating activity in support of the building up of the bodily organism and its functions. This especially concerns the lullabies.

Mood of the Fifth with Central Tone A

Pentatonic melodies can only move in a swinging motion around a central tone. They float, without a stressed beginning and without tending toward a resolved end. They expand in a spiral or in increasing struggle and constantly swing back within their own boundaries. They play with tones and are intoning play.
—Fritz Jöde

Mood of the fifth with central tone a′ corresponds to the cosmic experience of the child in the first seven years, who still is at one with the world and does not yet feel a polarity between it and himself. This musical mode forms a protective shelter in which the child can feel secure.

Mood of the fifth signifies unity with the cosmos, in which heavens and earth are yet united. It means being in harmony with a divine center. It is a tonal space of optimal balance. All tones of the upper and lower fifth intervals are equally far removed from the central tone a′. The entire space comprises not an octave but a ninth-interval in which everything is in balance. (See following diagram.)

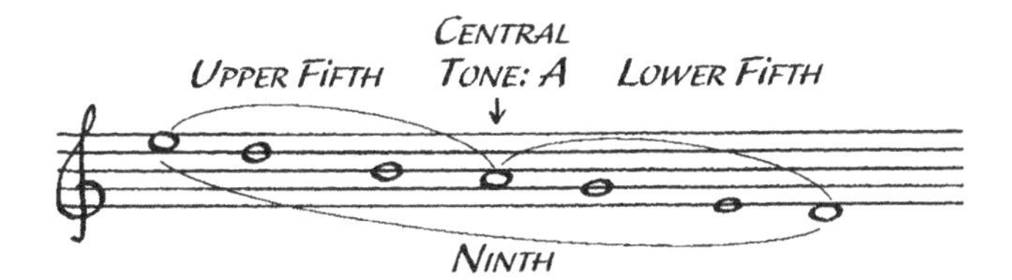

The diatonic scale has a different structure: there are two centers. Contrast is established between the fundamental tone and its octave. Half-tones, minor and major thirds give rise to minor and major modes with their respective feminine and masculine characters. From this springs the phenomenon of duality with the world, contrasting with the unity achieved through the mood of the fifth. In the songs for the first seven years of life, this duality should not yet be broached.

The entrance of the third, major and minor, makes it possible for the human being to come to know his inner life, to comprehend himself within his feeling. This offers the possibility of imposing limits on oneself, which represents progress in development. It is not hard to see how harm can ensue if the tendency for self-limitation is promoted in a child, for whom unity with the world is the needed basis for healthy development.

In the lullabies this need of the children is fully and entirely considered. According to manifold experience, the exclusive presentation of mood of the fifth motifs and melodies, brings about a profound recovery and healing from the harmful influences to which the child is exposed in his or her surroundings.

Mood of the fifth—tonal space:

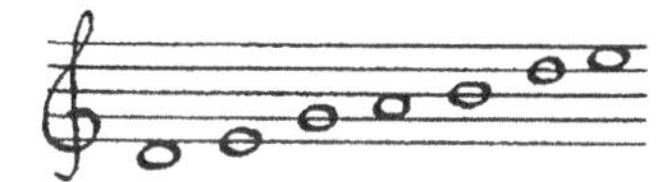

with the central tone a′ in its play about this central tone,

approximates the sound-gesture of rocking and brings about a dreaming, floating state of consciousness in the child. Sinking into the lower fifth interval

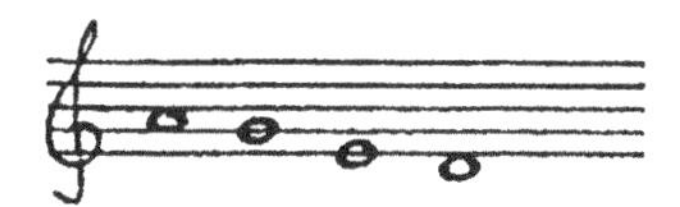

supports exhalation, yet allows return to the central a′ without too much heaviness, allowing freedom.

The experience of a light, floating sensation is supported by an upward climbing line:

In order to avoid "floating away," a gravitational counterpoise is given through final retum to central tone a′ —

—or through a play in second intervals around the central tone:

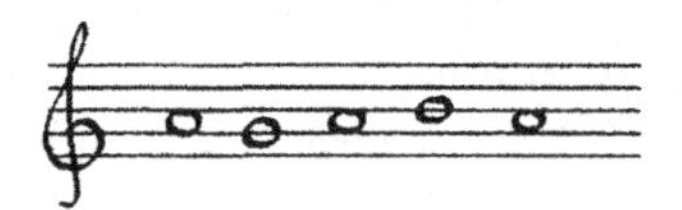

Born in 1921 in a small village on the shores of the Baltic Sea, as a young woman Wilma Ellersiek studied music, Dalcroze eurythmics, and speech, and taught for many years at the Stuttgart Music Academy. In her later years, following a serious illness, she turned to research on the effects of rhythm, language, and music on the young child, and out of this impulse she began to develop the songs, verses and "gesture games" that have been collected and translated in Giving Love—Bringing Joy *(WECAN, 2003) and its companion volumes. She died in 2007.*

Musical Forces and the Mood of the Fifth

RENATE LONG-BREIPOHL

The following excerpt from Chapter Eight of Under the Stars: The Foundations of Steiner Waldorf Early Childhood Education *by Renate Long-Breipohl is included with the kind permission of the publisher, Hawthorn Press. This excerpt is preceded by quotations from the book's introduction which lead us into the section from the chapter entitled "Art Experiences in Early Childhood Education."*

From the Introduction

Modeling and music play a special role in early childhood education. These art forms mirror the two major spiritual forces which determine growth and learning in early childhood: the etheric "formative" forces and the soul-spiritual "musical" forces, the former being closely related to the activity of modeling, the latter to rhythm and music.[1]

* * *

Special mention needs to be made of Steiner's recommendations for music education in the early years. His comments on the relevance of the intervals, specifically his comments on the "mood of the fifth," have inspired a fundamentally new approach to the musical education of the young child.

Following Steiner's lifetime, and especially after the 1960s, a number of musicians, singers, and instrumentalists have worked with Steiner's insights and composed music for young children, songs of everyday life, which bring the "mood of the fifth" into early childhood education. This is an ongoing process, as it is not easy for educators to embrace the kind of refined, objective musical quality in which Steiner wanted young children to be immersed. It places high demands on the teacher, including the training of hearing, quality of voice, and musical expression.

Steiner's approach to musical education is unlike any other and contrary to what would satisfy the musical taste of most contemporaries. It requires teachers to for-go their own musical preferences as adults for the sake of laying foundations in the child: foundations which will unfetter the child from tradition in musical taste and enable him to express himself in a musically creative way at a later age.[2]

Musical Forces and the Mood of the Fifth

Throughout early childhood, soul-spiritual forces envelop the child, forming a sheath through which the child is united with the souls of the people closest to him. Part of these soul-spiritual forces have also been at work within the child in the process of learning to speak, and subsequently remain within the child, especially in the lower part of the body. Steiner calls these soul forces "musical forces." Musical forces are connected with the will nature of the human being. We can perceive their effects in the movements of the child, specifically in the the young child's physical response to rhythm and beat.

According to Steiner there are powerful forces at work which should be left alone in early childhood:

> *These other forces come from outside. Forcing their way through the sculptural forces and descending into the organism, they co-operate in what takes place, beginning with the seventh year, in the building up of the child's body. I can characterize these forces in no other way than as those active in speech and in music. They are forces of a musical nature, which we take up from the outer world.*[3]

In perceiving tones and music the human being is able to form a connection not only to the natural and human environment but to the spiritual realm as well. When singing, for example, we may have the experience of the body acting as a musical instrument, the tones resounding through it as if the human being were an instrument for the music entering from somewhere else.

A single tone, melody, and harmony are experienced within the whole human being: body, soul, and spirit. The ear is the organ that receives the tone, but the actual experience of tone arises within the human soul. As Steiner puts it, the ear is a "reflecting apparatus for the sensation of tone": the actual musical experience occurs within.

The experience of music within the body is closely linked to the system of movement in the lower body. Steiner points out that the musical element, being related to the human limb system, can pass over into dance. This holds especially true for the young child: "The musical element that lives in the human being from birth and that . . . finds particular expression during the third and fourth years as an inclination to dance, is inherently a will element carrying life within it."[4]

These musical forces of the lower body exert such a strong influence on the child that he may be unable to control the resulting rhythmical movements of his limbs. Early childhood educators know from experience that music with a strong, pounding beat has such an effect on young children that they can move themselves into a frenzy and throw the entire group into chaos.

Bringing Musical Experiences to Young Children

Some important principles of early music education in Steiner early childhood education:

- Music should be brought to the young child gradually, in accordance with the process of incarnation.
- Music should meet the child's natural liveliness but also bring order to the child's will forces.
- Music and the world of tone should be introduced to the child through singing and the element of melody, not through harmony or beat.
- Care should be taken to protect the child's natural fine perception of tone from exposure to harsh, loud sounds and to avoid strain on the vocal chords caused by loud and low singing.

Musical education has to take into account the nature of consciousness in the child's early years. Much of the Steiner curriculum is based on Rudolf Steiner's insight that the development of consciousness in each individual child mirrors the development of the consciousness of humanity. In different cultures and at different points in time the experience of musical intervals evoked different soul experiences in human beings. In his work on the evolution of music,[5] Steiner tells how in ancient times, music based on the interval of the seventh would have brought about a spiritual out-of-body experience. Later on, the interval of the fifth would have been experienced as surrounding the physical human being. As of the Renaissance, the interval of the third, which has since dominated Western music, would call up an inward experience in the human being.

The interval of the fifth has played a major part in the traditional music of parts of Asia, and in the form of pentatonic music it was the major musical experience in Greece and then in Europe all through the Middle Ages.

What Steiner calls the "mood of the fifth" and recommends for the musical education of young children is based on elements of the early pentatonic music. It is characterized by the absence of harmony, musical scales and triads, which are so prevalent in post-medieval music. Melodic patterns move around a central tone rather than a base note or tonic, and songs are experienced as open, light, joyous and emotionally neutral: neither sad nor melancholic nor exuberant.

As a result, songs in the mood of the fifth have qualities that match the developmental stage of the young child. Young children are still in the process of taking hold of their bodies, of incarnating. The inner life of the soul is still undeveloped. We could describe the situation of the child as being spiritually between heaven and earth. Music based on the interval of the fifth mirrors this in-between stage, whereas music based on scales with emphasis on the tonic conveys a more downward, earthly quality.

Steiner suggests that songs in the mood of the fifth should be part of musical education up to school age, or even up to age nine: "Though it is not readily admitted, the child essentially dwells in moods of fifths. Naturally, one can resort in school to examples already containing thirds, but if one really wishes to reach the child, musical appreciation must be based on the appreciation of fifths; this is what is important."[6] Steiner has only given brief indications on the importance of the mood of the fifth, but since his day, musicians have developed his ideas. Not only have they created songs for young children in the mood of the fifth, they have also developed and worked with instruments such as the children's lyre, which conveys the quality of free floating, objective tone. The tone of the lyre fills the surrounding space but does not put demands on inwardness of soul, a quality not yet developed in young children.[7]

Moreover, early childhood educators have understood that the mood of the fifth is not limited to musical experience as such but characterizes the entire atmosphere that should prevail around young children so that they are immersed in the qualities of this musical mood.[8]

As already mentioned, for the young child music and movement belong together. Beat and rhythm are the elements of music that the child experiences most strongly. The element of beat can have such an impact on the will of the child that it leads to an uncontrollable urge for frantic movement.

Rhythm is very different. According to Steiner one has to use the musical element in teaching from an early age, but one should look more at the liveliness of rhythm rather than the content of music. With that, one will establish a good foundation for the strength of the will.[9]

Melody, with its rhythmical flow, is the main means of musical education in early childhood, and the human voice is the main instrument. Thus singing and movement belong together; the rhythmical flow of song speaks directly to the child's will, and by focusing on the ever changing rhythm rather than the repetitive element of beat, the will can become harmoniously engaged without getting overexcited. In order to provide such experiences the adult needs to cultivate a singing voice as well as learn to work with the child's natural urge to move and dance.

> *The musical element that lives in the human being from birth and that . . . finds particular expression during the third and fourth years as an inclination to dance, is inherently a will element carrying life within it. Yet strange though this may sound, in the way it expresses itself in the child to start with it carries life too strongly, life that is too stunning and easily benumbs consciousness. This strong musical element very easily brings about a certain dazed state in the child's development. Therefore we have to say: The educational influence we exert by using the musical elemcnt must consist in a constant harmonizing . . . something that is alive in the highest degree in the musical element has to be damped down so that in music it does not affect the human being too strongly. This is the feeling with which we ought to bring music to the children.*[10]

Since the early days of Steiner kindergartens these recommendations have been applied in the work with movement, song and speech in the daily morning circle, and also in the weekly eurythmy session provided by a trained eurythmist.

When singing with young children, the simplicity of song is important.[11] Simple melodies based on two, three or five tones are most appropriate and, provided they have a lively rhythm, the child will not get tired of them.

Steiner emphasizes that teachers must perform songs well. The quality of the teacher's singing voice is important because the child at this age is an imitator. It will make a difference whether the child hears a pleasant sound, a tone sung with ease and lightness, or a tone forced out from stressed vocal cords. Not that teachers have to be singers, but they do need to be sensitive to using the appropriate pitch (higher than the average adult pitch) and to matching the lightness of children's voices. A teacher's voice needs to sound softly so that young children, who are imitators, do not strain their own voices and thus damage their vocal chords.

> *To begin with, in the first seven years of life, the child learns everything by imitation, but then the child should learn to sing out of the inward joy experienced in building up melodies and rhythms . . . You must have the feeling that, while singing . . . every single child is a musical instrument and inwardly senses the pleasant feeling of sounds.*[12]

The daily singing should be valued by the teacher as practicing an art and should serve no other purpose than the experience and enjoyment of music.

Music is not a means for enticing children to do something they may not want to do, such as tidy up, come in from outside, or follow rules. In such cases the spoken word would be more appropriate. There is a difference between a song sung before story time in order to settle children and a song that captures the essence of a story just told and thus concludes story time. There is also a place for songs that prepare the child inwardly for the next step to come, or a song of grace at the beginning of a meal. There is a fine line between using music for purposes foreign to its nature and letting it take its rightful place as an art through which a mood appropriate for the education of the young child is established.[13]

Notes

1. From Renate Long-Breipohl, *Under the Stars* (Stroud, UK: Hawthorn Press, 2012) p. xxx.
2. Ibid., p. xxxi. The following excerpts are from pages 147 to 152 of the same book.
3. Rudolf Steiner, *Balance in Teaching* (Spring Valley, NY: Mercury Press, 1990), p. 19. With respect to musical education in the time between ages seven and fourteen Steiner states, "The astral body becomes emancipated between the change of teeth and puberty. And what emerges out of the essence of music forms humankind and makes them independent beings. No wonder, then, that the *music teacher who understands* these things, who *knows that human beings are permeated through and through with music*, will quite naturally allow this knowledge to enrich the singing lesson andthe teaching of instrumental music. This is *why we try not only to introduce singing as early as possible into the education of children, but to allow those with sufficient aptitude to learn how to play a musical instrument* so that they have the opportunity really to grasp the

musical element that lives in their form as it emancipates." From *Human Values in Education*, lecture of 24 July 1924, quoted in Michaela Glöckler, *Education as Preventive Medicine* (Fair Oaks, CA: Rudolf Steiner College Press, 2002), p. 203.

4. Rudolf Steiner, *Practical Advice to Teachers* (London: Rudolf Steiner Press, 1976), p. 47.

5. Rudolf Steiner, *The Inner Nature of Music and the Experience of Tone* (Hudson, NY: Anthroposophic Press, 1983), esp. chapters 5 and 6.

6. Ibid., p. 58.

7. Mention should be made of the book by Rita Jacobs, *Music for Young Children* (Stroud, UK: Hawthorn Press, 1991); and Julius Kneirim, *Quintenleider: Music for Young Children in the Mood of the Fifth* (Fair Oaks, CA: Rudolf Steiner College Press, 1994).

8. The UK journal *Kindling* has devoted a recent issue (19, 2011) to music for young children and how to work with the mood of the fifth in everyday kindergarten life. See especially articles by Sally Schweizer (reprinted in this volume) and Jill Taplin.

9. Rudolf Steiner, *The Spiritual Ground of Education* (Great Barrington, MA: Anthroposophic Press, 2004), p. 62.

10. Steiner, *Practical Advice to Teachers*, pp. 47-48.

11. Julius Kneirim has created a wonderful resource of such songs (see note 7). Recently Karen Lonsky has published a collection of work songs which she has composed in the mood of the fifth: *A Day Full of Song* (Spring Valley, NY: WECAN, 2010).

12. Quoted in M. Glöckler, *Education as Preventive Medicine*, p. 205.

13. Art itself must play its proper part in education and should be practiced free of purposes which are not intrinsic to art itself. In: Rudolf Steiner, *A Modern Art of Education* (London: Rudolf Steiner Press, 1972), p. 192f.

Dr. Renate Long-Breipohl advises and lectures around the world in early childhood education. She has taught kindergarten, and helped pioneer Waldorf education in Australia, and represented the Australian Steiner Kindergartens on the International Association for Steiner Waldorf Early Childhood Education. Her book Under the Stars *originated from her work with young children, research, lecturing, and from engaging with Rudolf Steiner's educational thinking and philosophy.*

Music for Young Children

RITA JACOBS

In these excerpts from her book Music for Young Children *(published by Hawthorn Press, now out of print) Rita Jacobs offers us inspiration "to do justice to the needs of young children" by developing our own understanding of music and its relation to human development. She explains how music feeds the child's soul and assists child development.*

From the Introduction

In their development, our children—especially when they are young—are dependent on our sensitive awareness and understanding of what to them are the realities of life. But often our apparently superior cleverness seems to be a hindrance to our healthy perception of the little child and our feelings appear governed by personal and superficial motives. Consequently, our intentions to cultivate musicality in educating our children all too often fall prey to our own tastes—our own likes and dislikes.

How can parents, or those in charge of young children who wish to foster music according to each child's stage of development, find helpful guidance?

This is possible first of all through an honest objective observation of the child. Such observation requires a certain maturity in the observer: if we easily give in to the child's wishes and apparent needs we fall into the fatal error, which happens so often nowadays, of always allowing the child to choose. We are then failing to recognize that the child's powers of judgment are as yet undeveloped and that, consequently, young children are unable to form their own opinions. The fallibility of such a permissive attitude would become obvious if we were to allow children to eat whatever and however much they might wish; for their very existence, children depend on our loving guidance. If we wish to do justice to the needs of young children, our upbringing of them clearly demands an inner maturity.

This maturity, or deeper self-knowledge, is not a question of age, nor can it be gained entirely from books, but there are many helpful guidelines available in Rudolf Steiner's anthroposophy with its extensive literature.

About the Origin of Music and the Human Being

Neither the origin of music, nor the origin of man's soul and spiritual nature, can be found in the sense-perceptible realm, in the "here and now." Yet music, this special gift to mankind, is the sounding expression here upon earth of mankind's spiritual development and soul.

Scientific research of musical history leads us back to approximately 3500 BC. It shows that the music of that time was nourished by the deepest wisdom emanating from the divine worlds, but its audible results would sound very primitive to our modern ears, at least when compared with contemporary standards. During the height of Chinese culture around 3000 BC, certain intervals[1] and definite tones belonged to each particular month of the year and governed all music activities. The same applied to the pentatonic[2] mode which, apart from the temple rites in which music played a dominant role, was certainly also known in ordinary life, although this is not specifically mentioned in musical history. At this time, the human being's total dedication to the spiritual was considered to be of fundamental importance. It is interesting to note that even today the Chinese language has no word corresponding to our word "I."

Five-tone music (the pentatonal music of Chinese high culture) is based on the interval of the fifth and, by its own nature and without needing any further elaboration, is entirely melodious and harmonious in character. It lacks the semi-tone intervals and the more rigid structure of our diatonic scales.

During the height of Greek culture (from c. 800 BC), twenty-four rhythmical[3] forms were used, initially for the spoken word and not yet for music. In those times music was subservient to spoken language, but these rhythmical variables of speech gradually found their way into music instrumentation. The interval of the fourth[4] determined the Greek scale-forms, which each—if experienced and played from above downwards—had a central tone, called the "mese" or "repercussa," in relation to the beginning and ending notes.

> *All good melodies have their middle note (mese) and all good composers use it frequently. If they should neglect it, they soon enough return to it more than to any other note.* —Aristoteles in his *Problems*

In the Gregorian[5] style of the Middle Ages this form of scale was still used. The first examples of polyphonic[6] music were the parallel octaves[7] of the Greeks which were extended to include parallel fifths and fourths during the course of centuries, to form the first harmonic[8] structures.

It is interesting to note that at the time of Christ's life on earth the innate experience of the direction in music—from above downwards—became reversed, leading to upwards from below. Even though the principle of the middle tone (mese) remained in use during the Gregorian period, a greater orientation towards the "ground-note" (or tonic) became more and more apparent in the music literature handed down to us. The sevenfoldness of the scales of the so-called "Church modes"[9] determined the music of those days. Its melodic, harmonic and rhythmical forms became richer and more varied, but a separation between church and secular music did not become noticeable until the time of the medieval "minnesingers." During the fourteenth century, a leaning towards the use of the interval of the third[10] gradually developed, although in the early stages this interval was still experienced as a dissonance. Only in the sixteenth century was the third fully accepted as a harmonious interval.

In the fourteenth century, by means of accidentals[11], the seven diatonic[12] tones were augmented and/or diminished. In this way, a twelve-tone tonality was developed out of the previous sevenfoldness of the scales.

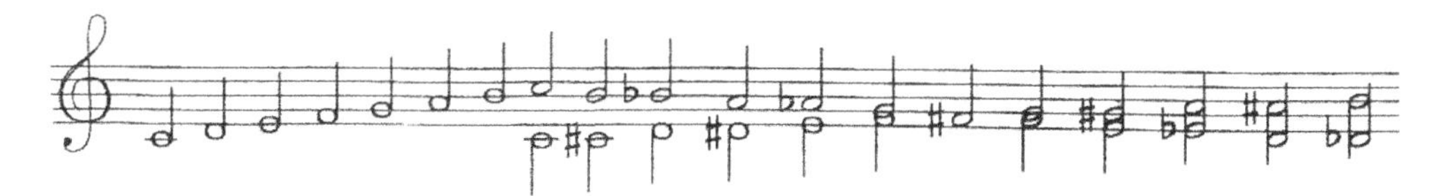

At this time the fullness of the music began to express itself in all its glory. The musical richness and virtuosity of the sixteenth, seventeenth and eighteenth centuries is still deeply impressive for us today. It was a time of freedom and development of different rhythms and measures. (The bar line[13] in music notation is found only in music written from the seventeenth century onwards.) All triads[14] were played as arpeggios[15], like a rustling wind. About two hundred years later it was Beethoven who expressed the compact power of whole towers of triads in his symphonies in an entirely new and different way from that of the earlier masters such as Handel, Bach, Haydn and Mozart. The possibility of expressing jubilation as well as deepest sorrow in music became more and more polarized and powerful.

In the music of the Romantic period, the experience of personal grief and pain was most forcefully expressed. Wagner's *Parsifal* was composed at that time, manifesting the awakening of the "I" out of forces of consciousness. In impressionistic music, the conglomeration of different chords dispersed again, leading to Schoenberg's intellectual twelve-tone music. Music continues to proceed along new ways.

These very short and aphoristic indications may serve as a glimpse into the evolution of mankind, revealed through the senses in the medium of music. Just as music became incarnated during the course of millennia, at first using only a few musical notes, so the soul-spirit of the child gradually becomes incarnated in the growing body. If we try to follow this development, we will begin to realize why the musical element plays such an important part in the child's developing soul life. On a miniature scale, the child undergoes similar stages of development to mankind throughout the millennia.

If we take seriously what has been accomplished by humanity in the field of music, and if we take the child's development seriously, we must realize that it is by no means a matter of indifference *what kind of music* we offer to young children. At the same time—and surely not for the last time—we wish to stress that the layman in music can definitely act correctly as an educator.

In the same way that music cannot be seen as the product of chance, neither can a newborn baby ever be considered merely as the result of chance. It is inconceivable that a newborn human being should have come into existence "only here on earth," that is solely through the fertilization of the maternal ovum. Again and again we are very deeply touched when we see the charm and magic of a little child. We clearly feel that the world of this child is not the same as our world. But what kind of world is it in which these little children of the earth are so clearly at home, while submitting themselves so trustingly to our care?

Again and again we can experience how we can reach these children, living in their own different world, if we offer them suitable music either sung or played on an instrument which needs to be in keeping with the child's still tender physical condition. We can then have the happy experience of witnessing how these little ones, on hearing our musical sounds, suddenly respond with an almost fully-physical listening. This seems to show us that music must have come from the same original home as the human being's soul and spirit. Since soul and spirit can only gradually find their way into the physical body, and because the memory of the spiritual home so recently left behind is still so alive, such music can be deeply meaningful to the young child. Here we are not thinking of the kind of music which encompasses the wealth and sophistication of adult tastes. Above all, we are not alluding to the mechanical sounds of electro-acoustic machines which for many adults have become indispensable for the stimulation of their nerves and senses. The tender physical organization of the child—if it is to develop healthily—is by no means robust enough to cope with such stress. Parents must be aware of what they do to their babies when leaving canned music switched on in the home, or when they even put them in front of the television screen in order to secure some peace and comfort for themselves! When some young children react to excessive mechanical noises by crying, by aggressive behavior or inability to play peacefully, it may lead to them being shouted at or spanked, but if such misguided parents realized what they were doing, they might wake up in horror from their easy-going comfort.

So what kind of music is suitable for the young child? Even about a hundred years ago there would have been no need to write about it. The most natural kind of music was *singing*. During the last few decades this natural and beautiful human capacity has become stunted and well-nigh lost. Artificially produced noises are swamping people's hearing and people in turn have become more and more silent. The art of conversation has become impoverished and the once natural gift of singing is slowly being eroded, or almost forgotten.

Well-meaning parents once told me that, because they could not sing in tune, every night they played evening songs on their tape-recorder, sung by a famous singer, so that their child should go to sleep peacefully. Perfection of performance offered by technical means often hides the real truth: in this case the truth is that for little children it is not the perfection of performance that matters, but that the child's guardians should make the effort to sing and that their singing should be the outcome of their love for the child. However inadequate such singing may be in the ears of the world, for the child it will be a most beautiful and intimate experience, which it will want to imitate. Adults should summon up the courage to bare themselves to the child, irrespective of their musical gifts. When with others, adults should show enough tact and tolerance to appreciate someone's musical efforts even if the results are far from perfect. Much harm is inflicted by the barbarous practice of some educators who still today segregate the singers from the "growlers" and who mock children who can't sing in tune.

For very young children it is enough if we just sing to them. If one wishes to go further, one can introduce simple instruments, such as children's harps, the children's flute, handheld resonators, etc. One can alternate playing and singing or combine both. A sound-producing toy usually is meant to stimulate the child's faculty of hearing. However, when buying such a toy, the loudness, beauty or ugliness of its sounds must be carefully judged. Loud sound-producing toys are unsuitable for the very young in the same way that loud talking or loud music would be, or the sound of a machine. In every case, the sounds of musical toys should be produced by hand and *not* electrically.

At about the stage when the baby begins to grasp objects, quite contrary reactions to music can be seen. When a mother sings her regular "Good-night" song, the child may listen intently and, stimulated by the grown-up's voice, may try to join in, singing its first tones. On the other hand, the little one may suddenly make the maximum amount of noise, banging any object at hand with tremendous zest and vigor. As the child's former need for sleeping decreases, its awareness of what is happening in its surroundings increases, together with a new and energetic urge to "grasp" the world (here meant quite literally). This is the time when acquaintance with music becomes more differentiated: tones and melodies belong to the world of listening and dreaming, but the energetic grasping of "rhythm instruments" (be they a bunch of keys or cooking spoons) belongs to the side of life to which a child will surrender itself with great enjoyment, and with the active participation of its limbs. (If an adult's nerves cannot stand the "joie-de-vivre" of the very young, a "distraction-maneuver" will still have a prompt effect!)

The middle way between listening and acting, between giving and taking, between the inner and outer life, still has to develop out of these musical polarities. The child has by no means yet reached the musical major and minor experience and is still far from being able to experience musical harmonies. Nevertheless, simple musical means can be found to foster the first musical feelings in their seedlike state of development. True, even a little child has feelings, but these still echo the surrounding world and are more of the nature of imitation. They are always dependent on the child's surroundings, and because of this the way we behave to each other in the presence of a child is always important. If we set an example of love and uprightness, we provide the child with a greater feeling of security and a better foundation for soul development than through opposite ways of behavior.

This inner balance manifests itself musically in the interval of the fifth, and songs consisting of only two or three notes in fifths will satisfy the musical needs of the very young child. Here are three examples:

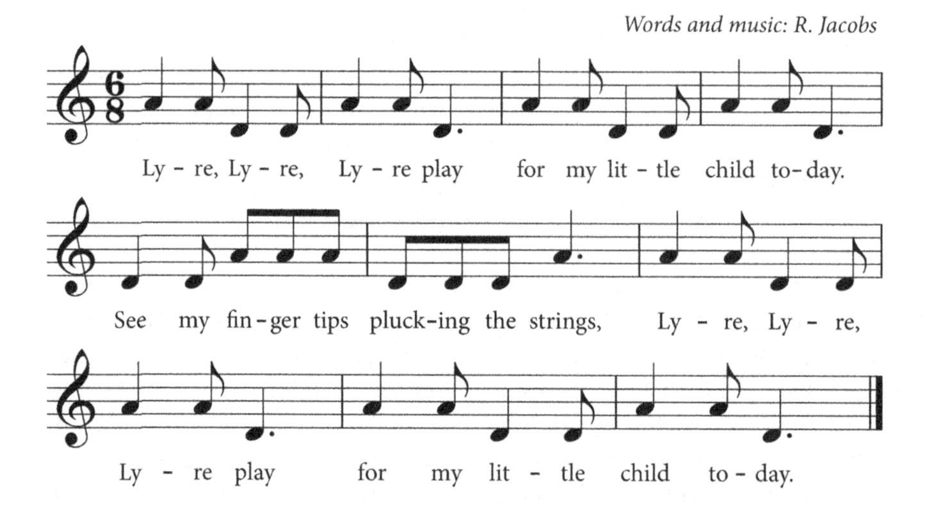
Words and music: R. Jacobs
Ly - re, Ly - re, Ly - re play for my lit - tle child to- day.
See my fin - ger tips pluck-ing the strings, Ly - re, Ly - re,
Ly - re play for my lit - tle child to - day.

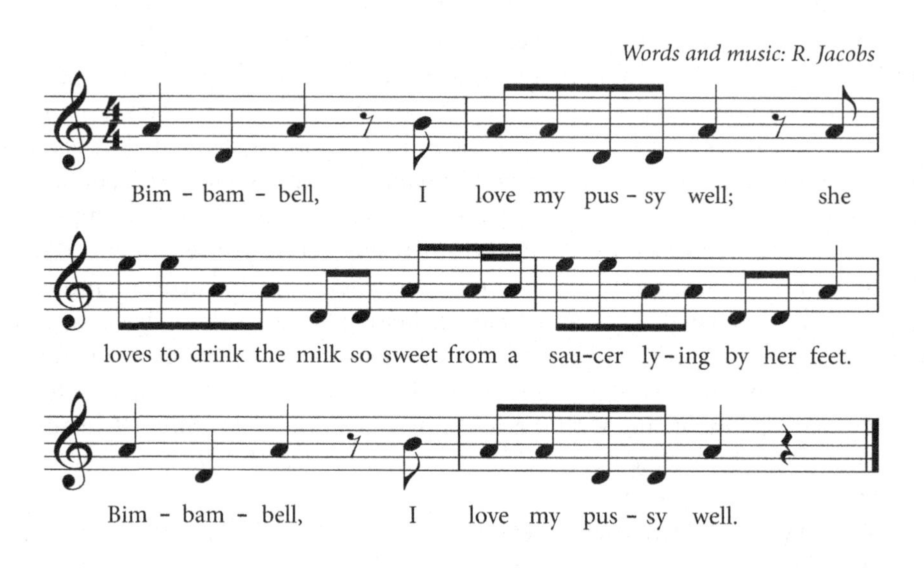
Words and music: R. Jacobs
Bim - bam - bell, I love my pus - sy well; she
loves to drink the milk so sweet from a sau-cer ly-ing by her feet.
Bim - bam - bell, I love my pus - sy well.

Words and music: R. Jacobs
3
3
Rick-et-y rock-et-y my old wain rum-bles up the hill a-gain
Who is in it, who rides home? Well it is my dar-ling John!

Even an adult, if allowing him- or herself to get involved in these two- or three-tone songs, may be captured by their innocent charm. Adults should try and compose similar simple songs: this is not as difficult as it may at first appear and it can be enormous fun! Repeat a little verse again and again until a simple melody suggests itself; when you have "caught" it, hold onto it and condense it so that it does not flutter away from the memory. Once it is safely written down, it can be sung to the child to whom such a little creation will be a special gift, even if it is only subconsciously received. As in the case of the earlier test of Courage (singing without a beautiful or trained voice), here again it is not just the result that matters, but the deed.

Notes (Glossary of musical terms)

1. Intervals: The distance from one tone to the next.

2. Pentatonic scale: A scale, comprising five tones only.

3. Rhythm: The nature of the movement of successive tones as they find expression in fast or slow, but also in measure and beat.

4. The Fourth: The distance from any tone to the fourth tone above or below within the diatonic scale.

5. Gregorian Music: Called after Pope Gregory (Pope from 590-604), the collector and composer of liturgical songs.

6. Polyphony: More than one melodic line being played simultaneously (i.e. in part-music). A round can also be considered polyphonic music, since the melody is sung or played after definite time intervals.

7. Parallel Octaves: A melody in unison, played either an octave above or below.

8. The first harmonic structure: The first, fourth and fifth interval of the scale, i.e. the prime, fourth and fifth, later on formed the framework of our harmonic System as: Tonic, Subdominant and Dominant.

9. Church Modes: The eight diatonic tones from the first to the octave (from c′ to c″, d′ to d″, e′ to e″, etc.) were the scales used for liturgical songs until the arrival of the major and minor scales. They are based on antique musical forms and appear as such in the older Byzantine Church Music, though not beginning with c′, but with d′ to d″, e′ to e″, f′ to f″, g′ to g″, etc. Church Modes received their names from ancient Greek provinces, such as the Dorian, Phrygian, Lydian, Mixolydian Mode, etc. Added to these there were the so-called secondary notes, a fourth below, i.e. from a to a′, b to b′, c to c′ and d to d′. Accidentals in the modern sense did not yet exist at that time.

10. The Third: The distance from one note to the third note of a diatonic scale, played either above or below the first note.

11. Accidentals: The augmentation of a half tone is prefixed by a sharp (♯) and the diminution of a half tone by a flat (♭).

12. Diatonic notes: The white keys on the piano keyboard.

13. Barline: Most of the music of the past four or five centuries falls into a regular scheme of beats (groups of two, three, four, etc.). For easier reading in rotation, the measures are marked off from each other by vertical bar lines.

14. Triads: Chords composed of thirds, for example : c′-e′-g′ (Tonic chord in the c major scale) f-a-c′ (Sub-dominant) and g′-b′-d″ (Dominant).

15. Arpeggio: Broken chord, the notes of a chord being played one after another.

Rita Jacobs has been director of an educational institute in Hamburg where she specialized in working with young children. She has investigated the origins of music and its life-enhancing nature.

Working with the Mood of the Fifth

JILL TAPLIN

This description of mood-of-the-fifth music leads us, by means of the piano keyboard, from the diatonic to the pentatonic scale, and then to the balanced character of the mood of the fifth.

All music creates mood, and music for young children should create a certain kind of mood. We might describe this mood as joyful, centered, simple, beautiful, ordered, calming, or flowing. We want it to encourage unselfconscious participation, in the words of one experienced Steiner/Waldorf educator.

As human evolution has brought about the awakening and contraction of consciousness, so musical development has evolved in parallel to this. Early European music, especially religious music, has a feeling of space and openness. For the past four centuries in the West, musicians have worked mostly with the major and minor diatonic scales, and harmonies have become closer and narrower. The nineteenth century Romantic movement has explored all the emotional possibilities of these major and minor scales in a rich and densely-textured way. Since then, there have been the atonal experiments of the past century and the explorations of micro-tones that electronic music makes possible. Our open, dreamy consciousness now wants to be woken up by close discords and intrigued by minute pitch distinctions.

But what do young children need, who still live in a dreamy and open state of consciousness? Before the diatonic scales, the simpler pentatonic scale was in use. This does not have any semitone steps and has a more open, expanded feel, matching the more expanded consciousness of earlier times.

On the next page is a picture of part of a piano keyboard. All the notes—white and black keys—on the piano keyboard are one semitone apart from their immediate neighbors. The first key on the left in this picture is the one often called "middle C," written in this book as c′ (the added symbol indicates the octave starting with this note). The names of the white keys in sequence from left to right are c′, d′, e′, f′, g′, a′, b′, c″ (starting the second octave), and so on.

So between the first key on the left, called c′, and the key called d′ next to it, there is a whole tone (two semitones) because there is a black key in between. There is also a whole tone between d′ and e′ for the same reason. But between e′ and f′ there is no black key, so they are only a semitone apart, not a whole tone. The same happens between the keys b′ and c″—they are only a semitone apart.

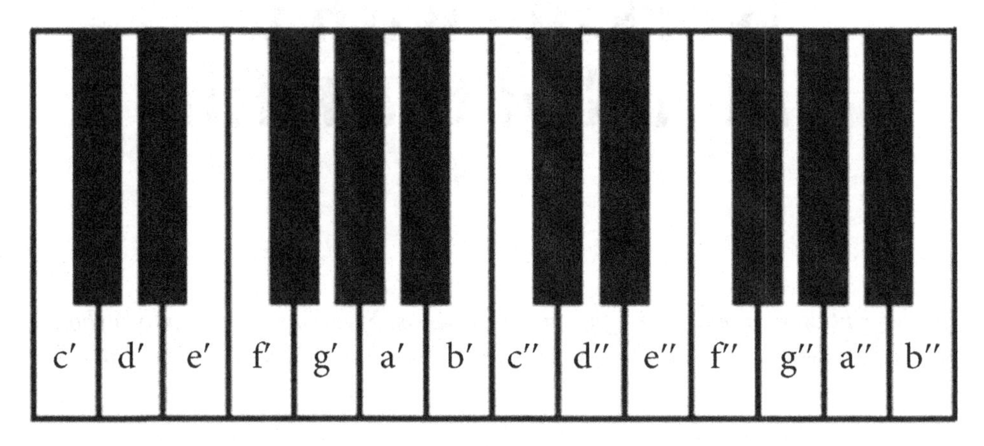

In the pentatonic scale you simply leave out the c′ and the f′ so that there are no notes closer together than a whole tone—no semitone spaces—and some of the notes are now a tone-and-a-half away from their neighbors. This "opens up" the mood of the scale, compared with the diatonic scale (such as the scale of C major). If you play (or get someone to play for you) the two scales shown below, you should be able to hear how much more open the pentatonic scale sounds—like a seascape or a moorland rather than a forest or a close-up of a flowery meadow.

Diatonic scale:

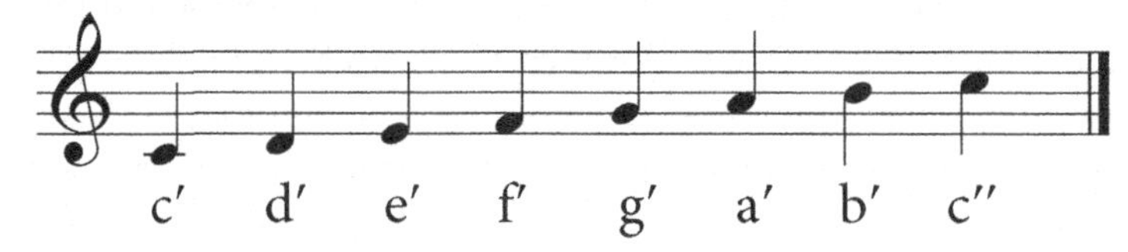

Pentatonic scale:

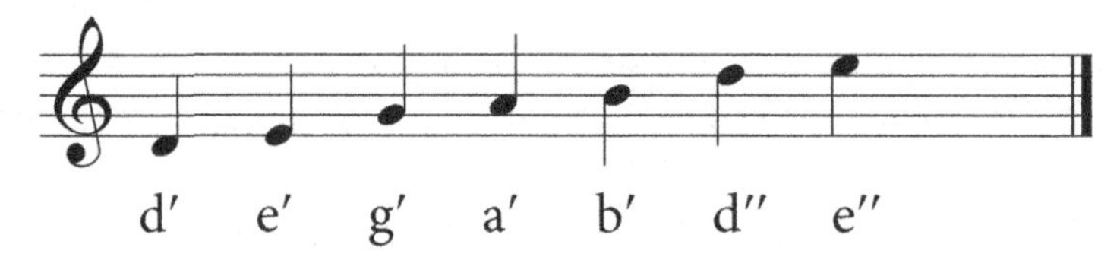

We find pentatonic music in folk music traditions, such as some Celtic music (the Skye Boat Song, for example) and some of the music of the twentieth-century Hungarian composer Zoltán Kodály. But music based on the pentatonic scale still has the tension of wanting to return to the key note, and it can still have the emotional content of major and minor intervals. You might feel these tensions in the second part of the Skye Boat Song, where it moves from a rocking melody to something more emotionally charged, as the words do.

Music in the mood of the fifth uses the notes of the pentatonic scale, but taking the a′ at the middle of the scale as the balancing note, with the melody rocking to the notes on either side of it and returning to it.

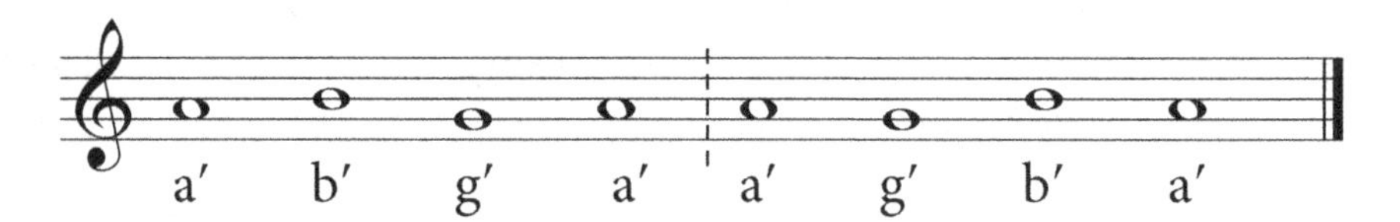

Or we may go further afield, to the fifth on either side but still remaining centered on the a′.

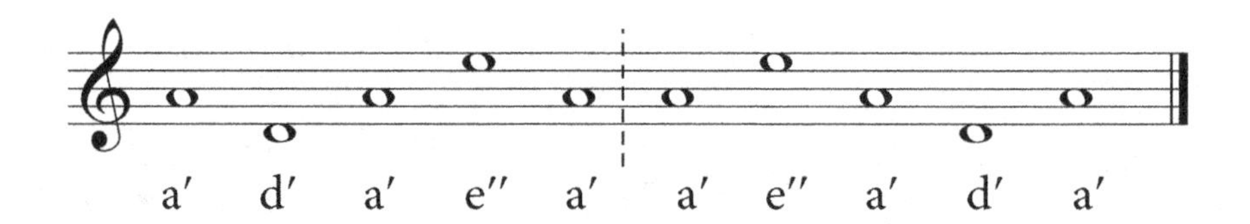

The other notes of the pentatonic scale can be used as passing notes but not with the emphasis that gives a major or minor feel, and the a′ remains the note to come home to.

Working with the mood of the fifth gives a feeling of more open possibilities than melodies which need to be resolved by returning to a key or "home" note at the bottom or at the top of the scale. This music has a very pure and simple feel to it, with a sense of objectivity rather than emotional content, in the same way as we tell stories. It is important to match this with a pure and natural singing voice. Children find the mood of the fifth easy and attractive to imitate; it encourages unselfconscious participation.

Rhythm is the other important element in music. It gives opportunities to bring in "color" by using polarities such as fast/slow, and to suggest movements such as stepping, dancing, or running. Look for the rhythms suggested by the words.

With the combination of the simple melody shapes of the mood of the fifth and appropriate rhythms, you can create songs of all kinds: circle times, snack blessings, and helpful transitional phrases. Here is an example for story time. Many others can be found in *Quintenlieder: Music for Young Children in the Mood of the Fifth* by Julius Knierim[1]; *Let Us Form a Ring* and *Dancing As We Sing*, both edited by Nancy Foster[2]; and other sources.

Children like traditional tunes too, but it is important to use some in the mood of the fifth if you can, because:

- This music is not individualized by minor and major intervals.
- Children have been awakened by the many kinds of music that they hear, but this music may help them to dream.
- Because this music is less fixed, it may help children to be more open to different kinds of music in the future.

It can be difficult for adults to become accustomed to the "empty" feel of this music. It will help if you practice it with colleagues and bring it to the children when you are comfortable with it.

Notes

1. Julius Kneirim, *Quintenleider: Music for Young Children in the Mood of the Fifth* (Fair Oaks, CA: Rudolf Steiner College Press, 1994).

2. Nancy Foster, *Let Us Form a Ring: An Acorn Hill Anthology of Songs, Verses, and Stories for Children* (Silver Spring, MD: Acorn Hill Waldorf Kindergarten and Nursery, 1989) and *Dancing As We Sing: Seasonal Circle Plays and Traditional Singing Games for Young Children* (Acorn Hill Waldorf Kindergarten and Nursery, 1999).

Jill Taplin is a kindergarten advisor as well as a teacher trainer. She has a particular interest in music, movement, and circle times in the kindergarten. At present Jill is based in Staffordshire, England, and works with trainings in Britain, Slovenia, Croatia, and Thailand.

The Mood of Early Childhood

Music in the Kindergarten

NANCY FOSTER

This article considers mood-of-the-fifth music in the context of the early childhood experience as a whole, and how this music supports the overall mood we wish to create in the early childhood classroom.

For inspiration in our work with music for early childhood, we may ponder Rudolf Steiner's statement that "song is an earthly means of recalling the experience of pre-earthly existence."[1] With this statement in mind, we will feel a responsibility to bring music into the early childhood setting not only with joy, but also with respect. How can we fulfill this responsibility?

Just as a plant has meaning and reality only in the context of earth and cosmos, so music and movement may best be considered in the context of the early childhood experience as a whole, by recalling the mood we are seeking to create in our classroom. We wish to provide an atmosphere in which the child can feel truly recognized as a being who has come into earth existence from a sojourn in the spiritual world. This is, of course, not spoken to the children, but the recognition is there in our thoughts, words, and deeds.

It is also our intention to nurture the quality of early childhood sometimes called dream-consciousness—a whole-hearted devotion to all that is in the surroundings, an un-self-conscious participation in life.[2] Rudolf Steiner tells us that ". . . the inner soul-being of the child, with all that he has brought down from pre-earthly life out of the world of soul and spirit, is entirely devoted to the physical actions of the other human beings around him. And this relationship can be described in no other way than as a religious one."[3]

The child's religious devotion is not the quiet inwardness we associate with the adult's religious devotion; certainly it *can* be a quiet condition, but it can equally well be lively and boisterous. It is the whole-hearted immersion in all that surrounds the child which is the characteristic quality we wish to encourage and support, in contrast to an analytical, self-aware approach in which the child senses a separation from the surrounding environment, a state of consciousness appropriate to a later stage of development.

We can support the child's immersion in the life around him or her—the quality of dream-consciousness or religious devotion—in a number of ways. In working with imitation, instead of instruction, we allow the child to enter into activities in a natural way. The child may imitate the adult outwardly—for example, making the same gesture; or, the child may simply absorb the gesture without doing it, but later imitate the gesture. For example, parents often tell us that their child has done all the circle gestures at home, though at school the child did not seem to participate at all. The child will also, however, imitate the inner activity or mood of the teacher. Our heartfelt involvement in whatever we do is taken up by the child, whether or not the child is outwardly imitating us.

We can further nurture dream-consciousness by bringing archetypal activities of life into the kindergarten, allowing plenty of time for creative fantasy play, and providing an environment of beauty and order. We seek to provide a rhythm for the early childhood day which will make dream-consciousness possible. This rhythm, most often described as in-breathing and out-breathing, could also be compared to a pleasantly rolling landscape. Hills and valleys are necessary and life-giving; but we hope to avoid dramatic precipices! Finally, our choice of music can be an important source of joy, of a healthy breathing rhythm, and a support to the child's natural tendency to enter activity with devotion.

Music and the Consciousness of the Young Child

The history of music is also the history of the incarnation and evolving consciousness of humanity. The human being's changing experience of self in relation to the cosmos finds an expression in the changing experience of music. In essence, it can be said that the human experience of music, and human consciousness itself, have moved from an expanded, less-incarnated condition, to one that is more contracted, more deeply incarnated.

Rudolf Steiner tells us[4] that in the time he designates as the Atlantean epoch, human beings were formed in such a way that the substance of their bodies was much more delicate than it later became. The human form was still mobile, and human beings were still given up to an experience of unity with the cosmos. The soul element stood in a different relationship to the world than that which we experience today. Human beings had no consciousness of the self as a separate entity; they experienced themselves to be "in god" rather than "in myself." At this time, Steiner tells us, music consisted of intervals of the seventh; human beings actually could not experience smaller intervals.

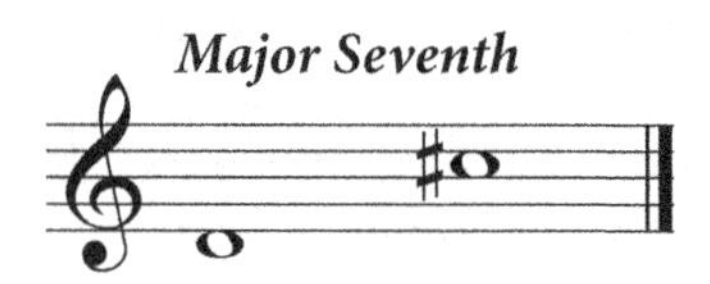

In the experience of the seventh, human beings felt transported into the realm of the gods. They did not experience themselves as making music; rather, their experience was, “I live in music made by the gods.”

In the Post-Atlantean age human beings began to descend more deeply into the physical body, and the interval of the seventh began to be “faintly painful.” They still felt at one with the gods, but to a somewhat lesser degree, so that the experience shifted from “I am in god” to “god is in me.” During this time, human beings developed a capacity for, and preference for, experiencing a sequence of fifths.

In the interval of the fifth, human beings still experienced a unity with the gods, but rather than feeling drawn out of their bodies in an exhalation, as in the seventh, they experienced both inhalation and exhalation, a breathing between inner and outer. They felt themselves to be “soul and spirit within their bodies.”

Experiencing the interval of the fifth, human beings felt, “The higher beings think, feel, make music in me.” This is, in fact, a description of the kindergarten experience of religious devotion to the surroundings, of being at one with the environment in a condition of total imitation or empathy, a breathing between inner and outer.

Eventually, in the fourth Post-Atlantean epoch, the “aptitude” for the interval of the third—major and minor—appeared.

The experience of the third calls forth an awareness of an inner condition, in which the human being feels the self within, distinct from the surroundings. Human beings thus felt that *they themselves* were singing; they felt themselves as earthly beings. In this way, humanity was gradually descending from the spiritual into the material world, and also, on the soul level, into a sense of individual selfhood.

Based on this overview of human evolution, we can see that music based on the experience of the fifth will meet the developmental stage of early childhood. We owe a great deal to the work of Julius Knierim, who brought this idea into practical application in working with children. Dr. Knierim used the expression “mood of the fifth” to characterize the experience of music based on this interval.

Music in the mood of the fifth swings or balances around the central note a′, creating a mood of purity, openness, and objectivity. This configuration of fifths can be presented as images:

Balanced motion around the a′:

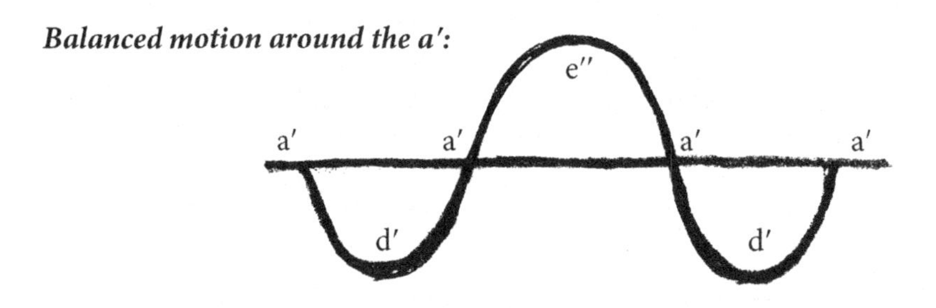

Lemniscate with a′ as center:

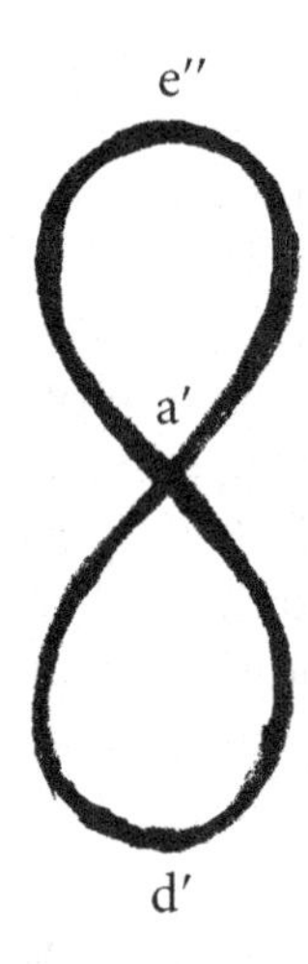

A melody based on the above images might sound like this:

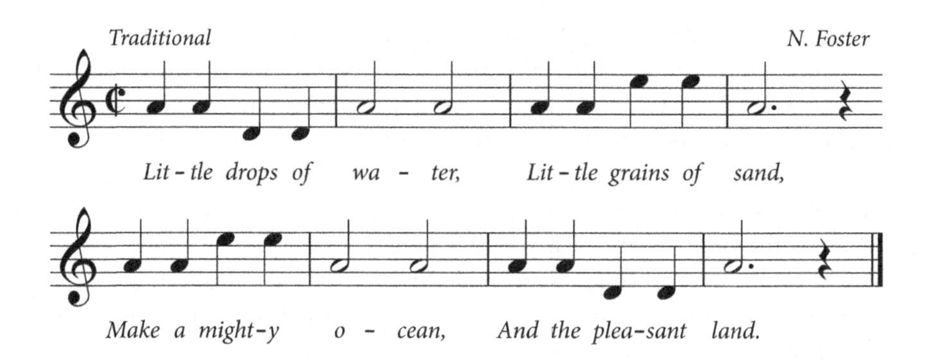

More varied, but still suitably simple, melodies can be created by adding other notes, still balanced around the a′ and still within the overall framework of the two fifths, a′ down to d′ and a′ up to e″. The notes g′ and b′ are most easily added. (A lower e′ and upper d″ can be used as passing tones, but care must be used not to contract the framework of two fifths—d′ to a′ to e″—into an octave—lower d′ to upper d″). Images for such melodies might look like this:

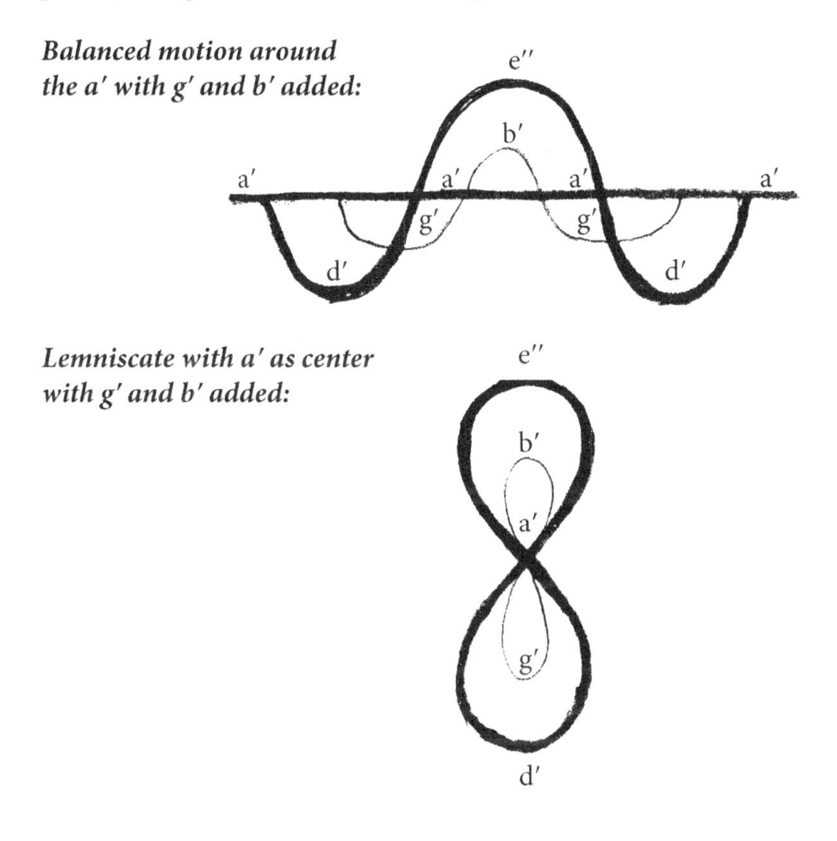

Balanced motion around the a′ with g′ and b′ added:

Lemniscate with a′ as center with g′ and b′ added:

Using the same nursery rhyme as above, we might then compose a melody that would sound like one of the following examples:

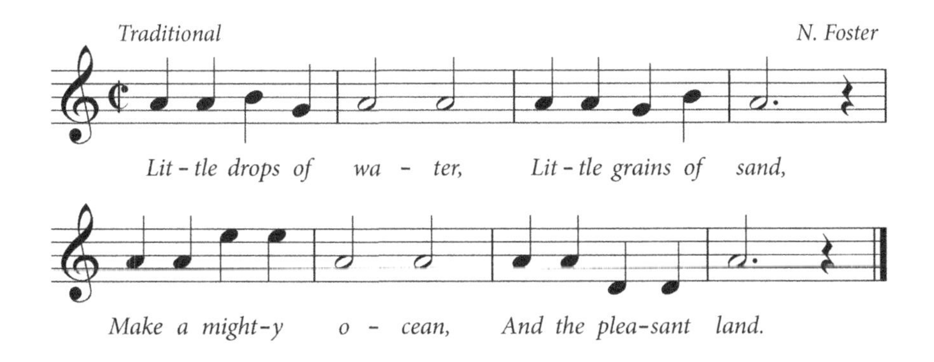

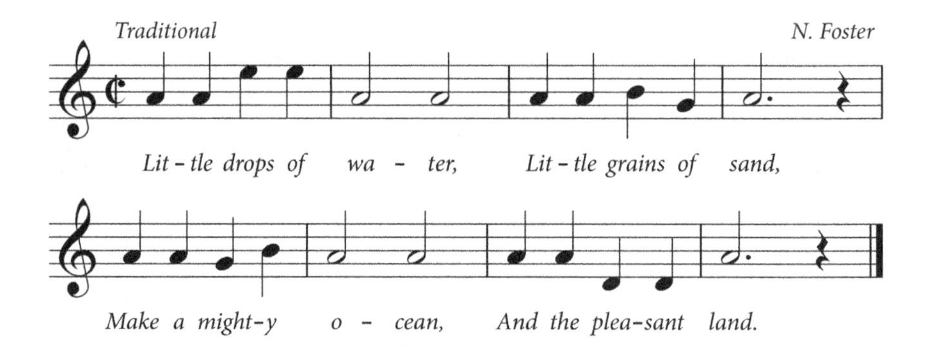

For adults, these melodies may seem strange or unappealing at first; it takes time to become used to their sense of purity and objectivity. They may even give us a feeling of emptiness. Bearing in mind our adult consciousness, this is understandable. Even for many children, this music in the mood of the fifth may not come easily at first, since they have most likely already been exposed to other kinds of music. In our times, we have all been bathed in a sea of tonality, so to speak, and this music based on fifths is very different. Nevertheless, if we understand the relationship of the mood of the fifth to the consciousness of the young child, we can see how important it is that children be allowed to experience this kind of music.

For those wanting to become familiar with music in the mood of the fifth, a helpful approach is to choose one song which you will sing with the children every day, perhaps at story time, or as a morning song at circle time. Gradually, as you become more comfortable with this kind of music, you may add more. The first step is to learn to understand why mood-of-the-fifth music is important for the young child; out of this understanding will grow the wish to become comfortable with it and introduce it to the children in your care. In the process, if the qualities of mood-of-the-fifth music are kept in mind, you can do much to bring this "mood" into whatever music you choose.

Songs based on the framework of the two fifths as illustrated above are in a suitable range for the young child's voice. For adults, this may present a challenge, but with practice, and by singing with a light "head tone," most people can achieve this voice range. It is a great help to the children's singing, and good training for their developing sense of pitch, if the teacher is consistent in beginning songs on the same pitch each time, as much as possible. If a correctly-tuned children's harp is kept nearby, for example, at least the first song can be started on the proper note. Even if the teacher is not able to maintain this through the whole circle play, it is at least a beginning. Adults' sense of pitch can also be developed! In any case, it is good to avoid slipping into a low voice range, since this is hard for children to imitate and often causes them to sing harshly.

The teacher's tone of voice can contribute much to the mood of the music. Singing in a clear, light tone will help to focus the children without overwhelming them. They will feel "invited" to sing and, just as in storytelling for the young child, dramatic effects will be avoided, so that a mood of joyful serenity will leave the children free to participate whole-heartedly in the music we bring.

Our own enjoyment of singing is a great gift to the children. As Rudolf Steiner said, "The joy of children in and with their environment must therefore be counted among the forces that build and shape the physical organs. They need teachers who look and act with happiness and, most of all, with honest, unaffected love. Such a love that streams, as it were, with warmth through the physical environment of the children may be said to literally "hatch out" the forms of the physical organs."[5]

In our striving to work with mood-of-the-fifth music, let us always remember to cultivate love and joy as we learn from the children what nourishes their devotion to all that is around them.

Notes

1. Rudolf Steiner, *The Inner Nature of Music and the Experience of Tone,* Lecture 4, Dornach, December 2, 1922 (Spring Valley, NY: Anthroposophic Press, 1983), p. 35.

2. Rudolf Steiner uses the term "dream consciousness" in the following passage from "Education and Spiritual Science," Cologne, Dec. 1, 1906, published in *The Education of the Child and Early Lectures on Education* (Great Barrington, MA: Anthroposophic Press, 1996), p. 66: "Our dream consciousness is a residue of the Atlantean's normal pictorial consciousness, which could be compared to what a person experiences in vivid dreams during sleep. But the pictures of an Atlantean were animated, more vivid than today's most fertile imagination. Furthermore, Atlanteans could control their pictures, so that they were not chaotic. We see an echo of this consciousness when young children play, endowing their toys with pictorial content."

3. *The Essentials of Education,* Stuttgart, Lecture 2, April 9, 1924 (London: Rudolf Steiner Press, 1982), p. 37. See also *The Child's Changing Consciousness as the Basis of Pedagogical Practice,* Lecture 3, Dornach, April 17, 1923 (Anthroposophic Press, 1996), p. 47.

4. See the lectures collected in *The Inner Nature of Music and the Experience of Tone,* op. cit., and also the lecture by Rudolf Steiner "Pneumatosophy: The Riddles of the Inner Human Being," Berlin, May 23, 1923.

5. Rudolf Steiner, "The Education of the Child in the Light of Spiritual Science," 1907, published in *The Education of the Child and Early Lectures on Education,* op. cit., p. 22.

Nancy Foster taught children and parents at Acorn Hill Waldorf Kindergarten and Nursery in Silver Spring, MD, USA, for over thirty years. Now retired from teaching, she serves as the Membership Coordinator of the Waldorf Early Childhood Association of North America and teaches in the part-time early childhood teacher education program at Sunbridge Institute.

PART TWO

Deeper Insights into the Mood of the Fifth

A Path of Discovery

Working with the Mood of the Fifth

DYANNE HARSHMAN

After inviting us to accompany her on a "path of discovery," Dyanne suggests that we become scientists in our work with music, enlivening our journey through our observations, questions, and reviewing, thus bringing an inner gesture that will bring nourishment to the children in our care.

Many years ago I entered the Waldorf kindergarten space as a parent seeking a healthy and wholesome education for my children. In a larger culture riddled with dis-ease and alienation, health and wholeness turned out to require parent education as well, and so I signed up to be a student of this appealing package. Among the many "first things" I noticed were the soft swirls of color on every wall, an interplay of light and pigment in movement that moved me deeply. The dollies lay peacefully nestled in their beds, all seemingly handmade and not one with a face! The shelves and corners of the room held beautiful shells, rocks, large tree cones, sanded stumps, and nicely folded cloths and silk—no buckets of Legos, stacks of puzzles, or factual posters that were common to other early childhood rooms. The first puppet play I attended displayed exquisite marionettes made of silk (with no faces) that moved with simple yet profound gestures while the puppeteers, seen by all, quietly gave them life, and the words of the storyteller became the translation of this finely-tuned movement of form, color, and light, luring me into the world of the unseen.

At our parent meeting in the fall, the teacher handed out music to a handful of songs that we would all learn and sing at our upcoming Lantern Walk festival. As a musician of many years, I felt ease and confidence with this task, feeling sure that I probably already knew some of these songs and could read the music of those yet unfamiliar. Not only was the selection all new to me, but each of the songs also resided in an unusual tonality. They were all pentatonic (using a five-note scale) and some even left the listener feeling somewhat suspended, as if led on a journey and held in the place of the "in-between." As the teacher carefully taught each song, I could sense that some great intention stood behind this carefully delivered musical experience. In all these experiences—the lazured walls, the dollies and puppets with no faces, and the unique musical mode—I felt opened up and invited into the world of the unseen. There was something deeply true in each of these experiences: a truth that I could feel but not intellectually explain. I could only surmise that whatever stood behind this whole form of education must hold something profound enough to stand on its own in the midst of the common mainstream.

Since that time, I have had the pleasure of teaching in such a classroom for sixteen years, spanning the ages of two through seven years. Indeed, there *is* something quite profound that stands behind all that we do. From our various trainings and conferences, we have all probably heard references to the early childhood teacher as "priest" and "artist:" that our constant exercise of creativity and beauty must be matched by our inner discipline toward non-sentimental love immersed in the archetypes. I believe we must also consider ourselves "pedagogues" and "scientists." We are given the framework of a model of human development that informs our work. We are given various indications as to what to bring to children at what age and how we might accomplish that. This alone, however, is not enough to fulfill the deeper mandate of a Waldorf education.

We must also become scientists in our work, observing, hypothesizing, testing, and reviewing, never ceasing to ask questions as a means of furthering our own discovery. This is what brings meaning to our work, enlivening it with inspiration and teaching us with the intuition that follows. This is also the inner gesture that will become deep nourishment for the highly imitative young children in our care.

With that in mind, I would like to make a case for taking quite seriously the musical indications for the young child given to us by Rudolf Steiner and others who followed. Such indications would lead us to the world of "the mood of the fifth," a kind of tonal and rhythmic arrangement that creates a mood of openness and breathability. If you are reading this article, the mood of the fifth is probably not a new concept to you. However, as is true with many anthroposophical ideas, new layers of understanding can be revealed throughout our lifetime, if we choose to study it further. Who really knows what the mood of the fifth is? This is an open question waiting to be worked over. And to take it up with any earnestness in our work with young children, we must place ourselves in active inquiry. Again, we must become scientists.

Over the years, I have observed my own at-first-unyielding antipathy toward the constant use of music in the mood of the fifth. To keep this mood of the fifth alive in all that I bring musically requires discipline, will, and faith. When I visit other classes in other schools, I observe the same inner struggle in many of my colleagues. Through observation and conversation, I have come to believe that there are a few hindrances, common to many of us, which keep us from easily taking this up with the seriousness it surely deserves.

I don't really know* what *the mood of the fifth is. Well, I'm not sure if anyone really knows for certain. But, there are a few pieces of information that can help give it context. Then, we can go from there into studying the qualities (and therefore the mood) of the actual interval of the fifth.

I don't know* why *I am doing this. The tonality of the mood of the fifth is often not very pleasing to the adult ear. It sounds empty and uninteresting. It can be quite boring, actually. It might even seem as though the children respond better to the familiar major and minor songs to which they so easily begin to sing along. In order to commit to the delivery of this very different kind of sound (and commitment is what is required), we must have a sense of the potential importance and meaning behind it, for that is where the seed of motivation for inquiry and further study lies.

I don't know* how *to approach this study. Having a basic understanding of musical concepts makes it easier to move about freely as we discover the nuanced differences between a diatonic, a pentatonic, and a mood-of-the-fifth song. Not having these concepts, or not feeling confident musically, can make it difficult to know if we are approaching the task adequately.

What Is the Mood of the Fifth?

The "mood of the fifth" is a phrase used to describe a mood that can be produced using a certain set of tones, usually seven tones that make up a pentatonic scale with two of the notes repeated in the next octave. To keep in the mood of the fifth (as contrasted to simply pentatonic), particular attention is paid to the sequence of those tones as well as the rhythm and beat patterns that eventually carry the melody line. It is a mood that is present when the interval of the fifth is sounded. To fully understand this, it is helpful to experience the interval of the fifth, to hear and recognize that sound and the qualities that exist within it. When doing so, it is nice to hear the tones separate from each other, as a melodic interval, and to also hear them sounded together, as a harmonic interval.

It is even more helpful to hear the fifth contrasted with the intervals of the major and minor third. We cannot do this in a written article. But you can take a moment to play these tones (or ask someone to play them for you) on the piano or other instrument. Reflect on your personal soul response to each.

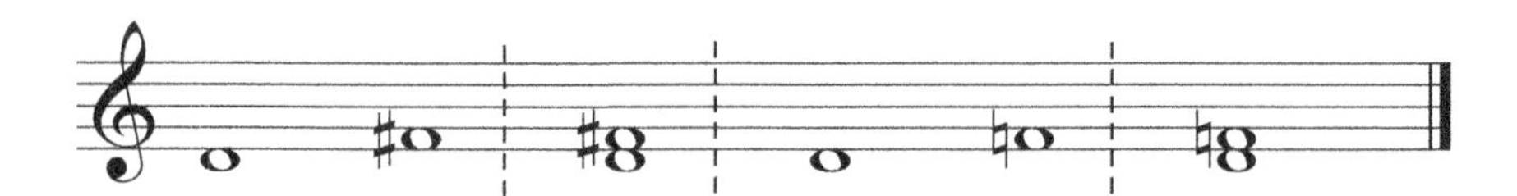

With that experience as your foundation, I would like to take us on a quick journey through the evolution of human consciousness, especially in light of these intervals. The esoteric relationship between intervals and human consciousness can serve as a framework for later defining (or attempting to define) the mood of the fifth. For the purposes of this article, our journey through these epochs will be brief.

I highly recommend a more detailed examination of this study, which can be found in Steiner's collection of lectures, *The Inner Nature of Music and the Experience of Tone.*[1] Hans Erhard Lauer also renders a helpful picture in his essay, "The Evolution of Music."[2]

It is easiest to begin with our current state of human consciousness, the development of Consciousness Soul, and our current ease and pleasure in music based on the intervals of the major and minor thirds. Most of the music of our time finds its resolution when the third is sounded. We know the song is done because it has landed in a way familiar and pleasing to our ear. This sensation of familiarity is predominantly based on an interval of either a major or minor third, and it has been the case since the early eighteenth century. Only in the last century has music begun to find resolution in the tighter and more dissonant interval of the second. Although this interval still carries a certain discord and uneasiness when heard, the human being has begun to develop a kind of newfound pleasure in its particular resonance. In the last hundred years, composers have gone out on a limb with such compositions as Stravinsky's *The Rite of Spring*, which, when first performed, caused riots in the audience, yet now is considered a masterpiece. According to spiritual science, this progression of pleasure of the dissonant interval of the second will continue to grow into the future until eventually the music based on the interval of the third will actually begin to feel somewhat painful. We are not there yet, but the description of this evolving human experience serves us well as we try to understand past epochs of human consciousness and their relationship to the musical experience.

The dawning of the fifth post-Atlantean epoch brought about the newly discovered pleasure in hearing music based on the intervals of the major and minor thirds. In Gregorian chant, we can trace back to a time when the tonal lines moved from a feeling of the fourth to a feeling of the third. Suddenly a certain duality presented itself for the first time: leaving the perfect fourth behind, there came the divided possibility of the major feeling or the minor feeling. Duality was a newly awakened soul experience. When human beings began to wrestle with this duality, music that rested on major or minor thirds began to feel pleasing.

We now experience this duality so strongly that it is difficult to remember our former Oneness. Here, it is good to take a moment to notice the similarities of soul experience between the sense of duality I have just described and that of the child going through the nine-year change: major or minor, duality, and the awakening of inner soul life.

Now let's go back a little further, into ancient Greece, where music that was pleasing rested on the interval of the open, objective fifth. In this music, thirds and fourths could be heard, but they were experienced as passing intervals on which the ear did not seem to rest. The human soul had not yet experienced itself in the qualities of major and minor thirds, so these intervals did not offer a sense of resolution. Rather, the ear would hear resolution when the fifth was sounded. This was most pleasing to the human being. At that time, the human soul still felt connected to the gods, while simultaneously having the newly awakened soul experience of being earthly and mortal. The ancient Greeks wove freely between the two worlds and produced, in the process, great works of art and philosophy.

The following are a few descriptions given by Steiner in lectures V and VI of *The Inner Nature of Music and the Experience of Tone*:

> *The experience of the fifth arose, and during this time man still felt united with what lived in his breath. He said to himself—though he did not say it, he felt it; in order to express it, we must word it like that—'I breathe in, I breathe out . . . .' Man always felt as if he were leaving and returning to himself in the musical experience. The fifth comprised both inhalation and exhalation.* [3]

> *. . . [W]ith the feeling for the fifth man actually feels transported.*[4]

> *. . . [W]hen he experienced fifths, he would have been inclined to say, 'The angel in my being is beginning to play music. The muse in me speaks.'* [5]

> *At that time the human being truly felt in the experience of the fifth, 'I stand within the spiritual world.' . . . Because he still possessed imaginative consciousness, he felt that the fifth, which he himself had produced, took its course in the divine realm. Man still had imaginations, still had imaginations in the musical element.*[6]

Hans Erhard Lauer describes such imaginative experience of the ancient Greek in this way:

> *[In imagination] pictures are in fact seen, but although made up of elements drawn from the physical world, they are not experienced in a purely physical way but rather as an expression or revelation of the supersensible beings and facts.*[7]

This time period of the ancient Greeks seems to reflect most accurately the consciousness of the young child today before the age of nine, and most especially before the age of seven, as we can see when considering what we know by our own observations of the young child: filled with imagination, living in the moment, and breathing in and out between the worlds of the earthly and the spiritual.

Why Am I Doing This?

Music holds a very special place in relation to the spiritual and physical beginnings of the human being. The source of resounding Tone and Word lies deep in the spiritual world. It is the creative force to which our connection is fundamental. It is said that human beings are created in the likeness of the Creator. This would mean that human beings are made up of Tone and Word, and are themselves creative beings. The human form is a finely tuned instrument of the music of the spheres. We don't *make* music. Music already exists. We *are* music. And as creative beings, we have the potential to transform ourselves, our relationships and our surroundings by way of vibration. With this in mind, music becomes something quite different than a mere art form.

According to Rudolf Steiner, music and visual art are two very different human experiences, whose sources of inspiration lie in different spiritual realms. Additionally, they each have a different impact on the human soul since they are experienced through different sensory gateways (mainly visual and auditory). At the risk of over-simplifying, we could say that the visual arts are a reflection of the interplay of light and color from the astral world, while music is a direct streaming from the Devachanic world. As a seer, Steiner describes this Devachanic world as lying behind the astral world, infused with its color but whose essence is tone: "That which was light in the great stillness [in the astral world] now begins to resound."[8] Furthermore, this world is described as man's spiritual home, the world in which we reside between lifetimes as well as the world which we visit each night while we sleep. Our connection to the Devachan is our spiritual lifeline, that which helps us to remember our spiritual roots.

In the previous lecture, Steiner said,

When man dwells within the musical element, he lives in a reflection of his spiritual home. In this shadow image of the spiritual, the human soul finds its highest exaltation of man. This is why even the most humble soul feels in music an echo of what it has experienced in the Devachan. The soul feels at home there. Each time he listens to music man senses, 'Yes, I am from another world!'[9]

The sensory experience of art and of music is also quite different one from the other. Fritz Julius describes this well in his book, *Sound Between Matter and Spirit*:

In seeing we usually direct our attention sharply toward the object. It is as if our innermost being reaches out towards it. The eye serves as a gate through which our soul enters the wide halls of light-filled space where it has many diverse encounters.

In listening, however, we open ourselves to what wants to enter us from our environment. Sound weaves around us; it is much less fixed to a specific place. Sound forces itself on us so that we have difficulty rejecting it. Sound often penetrates deeply into our organism, sometimes giving us pleasure and sometimes pain.[10]

The musical impulse is close to all human beings, and most especially to young children who so recently left that world of Tone to descend into their earthly bodies and the tasks therein. Furthermore, the musical experience has such a deep impact on body, soul, and spirit of all ages. Any indications of how we might use music in our work with children should therefore be considered with great care.

After lecturing about the evolution of human consciousness as it relates to the human being's relationship to different musical intervals, Steiner says to his audience:

All this is extraordinarily important when one is faced with the task of guiding the evolution of the human being regarding the musical element. You see, up to about the age of nine, the child does not yet possess a proper grasp of major and minor moods, though one can approach the child with them. When entering school, the child can experience major and minor moods in preparation for what is to come later, but the child has neither one nor the other. Though it is not readily admitted, the child essentially dwells in moods of fifths. Naturally, one can resort in school to examples already containing thirds, but **if one really wishes to reach the child**, *musical appreciation must be based on the appreciation of the fifths; this is what is important.* **One does the child a great kindness if** *one confronts it [the child] with* *major and minor musical moods as well as an appreciation for the whole third complex sometime after the age of nine . . .*[11]

How Do I Approach This Study?

As teachers, we put a great deal of time and intention into creating spaces and experiences that we believe will be nourishing and health-giving for the children in our care, based on our understanding of their needs. We bring stories filled with archetypes rather than explicitly-stated morals. We give the children full experiences of watery color in its purest state: movable, flowing, breathable, without instruction toward form. They care for dolls which do not burden them with a fixed facial expression. We meet their questions of curiosity with awe and wonder. When connecting with a child, we seek to meet him or her with a soft, open gaze. When meditating on the children and when in their presence, we strive to offer them our non-sentimental love, free of our judgments, opinions, and personality.

All this, and more, fills our hearts, minds, and will as an act of devotion to the children in our care. These are all qualities of the open interval of the fifth. We already offer children this mood in their environment, in the experiences we bring to them, and in our presence with them. Why, then, would we not put equal intention into the audible representation of this mood by giving the children mostly (if not exclusively) music based on the interval of the fifth? With the very same devotion, we can apply our will to the transformation of whatever hinders us from this task.

"***But if one really wishes to reach the child . . .***

. . . musical appreciation must be based on the appreciation of the fifths." To approach young children with a deep respect for their natural state of being, and then do all we can to preserve that state for as long as we can, is the least we can do. And, since the musical experience is one that connects us, too, to our spiritual homeland and reminds us of our spiritual roots, it seems only right to offer this to the children in a way that musically meets them exactly where they are and affirms the openness we wish for them to maintain as they incarnate. In this way a mood of the interval of the fifth can be one of our most profound tools for supporting the healthy incarnation of the child.

"***One does the child a great kindness if*** . . .

. . . one confronts the child with major and minor musical moods . . . sometime after the age of nine." This is no small statement, and deserves to be taken quite seriously, especially in this time when intellectualism and materialism prevail and children are not easily afforded a proper and wholesome childhood. To commit to an "appreciation for the fifths" and to holding off confronting the child with major and minor musical moods until "sometime after the age of nine" will require a great deal of resolve on our part as teachers. It will require that we set aside our own possible antipathies toward this form of music and commit ourselves to the work of understanding the mood of the fifth, using it with the children often and over time, and using our observations as research.

Notes

1. Rudolf Steiner, *The Inner Nature of Music and the Experience of Tone* (Spring Valley, NY: Anthroposophic Press, 1983).

2. Hans Erhard Lauer, "The Evolution of Music," in *Cosmic Music: Musical Keys to the Interpretation of Reality*, ed. Joscelyn Godwin (Inner Traditions, 1989), pp. 168-225.

3. *The Inner Nature of Music and the Experience of Tone*, pp. 55-56.

4. Ibid., pp. 55-56.

5. Ibid., p. 52.

6. Ibid., p. 62.

7. From Lauer, op. cit.

8. *The Inner Nature of Music and the Experience of Tone*, Lecture II, p. 16.

9. *The Inner Nature of Music and the Experience of Tone*, Lecture I, p. 8.

10. Fritz Julius, *Sound Between Matter and Spirit* (Spring Valley, NY: Mercury Press, 2005).

11. *The Inner Nature of Music and the Experience of Tone*, pp. 57-58, emphasis added.

Dyanne Harshman is a teacher and musician who was born and raised in the Pacific Northwest. She has performed a wide variety of musical genres including classical, folk, jazz, and most recently, Zimbabwean music, and holds a Master's degree in Waldorf Education. She has taught nursery and kindergarten at the Whidbey Island Waldorf School in Washington since 1998 and currently serves as adjunct faculty teaching music at Sound Circle Center for Anthroposophy.

The Mood of the Fifth

The Blessing of Wonder

LISA GROMICKO

Based on her studies of Rudolf Steiner's lectures and other anthroposophical sources, as well as her own experiences as an early childhood teacher, Lisa shares thoughts on the significance of mood-of-the-fifth music for the healthy development of the young child in today's world.

Today, many young children have become prematurely self-aware, awakening early from what can be called "dream-consciousness," that state of early childhood which Rudolf Steiner described as being "wholly sense organ"[1] and which ideally accompanies the first seven years of life. During these years, impressions of the world are taken in, and these impressions form the child's physical body, including the organs, brain and nerve-sense system, musculoskeletal and cardiovascular systems, and all bodily rhythms.

The Incarnating Child

Children come to us from the spiritual world and continue to be very connected to that world during the first seven years of life. Dream-consciousness allows the child to co-exist "between heaven and earth" as the important work of building the physical body and establishing the foundational senses takes place, providing the physical basis of human life and the later development of the Consciousness Soul.

Early self-awareness can have significant effects on this important work of the first seven years, interfering in profound ways. It nudges the young child from the warm, unconscious state of building the body—wholly sense organ, at one with the universe. Once awakened to self-awareness, the young child may begin to separate prematurely from this wholeness, and as a result of the awakened consciousness, formative life forces can be drawn away from building the physical body. Feelings of anxiety, as well as social challenges resulting from early judgment of self and others, can follow, and the child's sense of the world as being good and wholesome can suffer. Early self-awareness, before the capacity for conscious work on the self has developed, does not help the young child to incarnate, but rather can contribute to significant hindrances to healthy development.

Audrey McAllen encouraged early childhood teachers to help children to live in dream-consciousness in order to nurture the healthy formation of the physical body during the first seven years. She writes, "The kindergarten heals by helping the child to regain his dream consciousness stage from which he has been pushed out too soon. The kindergarten allows the formative forces to go back to their proper functioning in completing, as well as they are allowed, their bodily work."[2]

Rudolf Steiner describes the ways that the experience of music can affect the healthy development of the human organism: the nerves, breath, blood circulation, and rhythms of sleeping and waking. Musical forces, brought properly, affect the human being all the way into the will, either enabling or preventing the quality of courage, later in life. It is thus very important to consider what is musically healthful in early childhood and what can better wait until a later age. Steiner states, "Proper introduction to the musical element is fundamental for a human being to overcome any hindrance that impedes, later in life, a sound development of a will permeated with courage."[3]

Many children today experience great challenges in fully taking hold of their physical bodies. Several factors can be at work here. Do they feel "at home" on the earth? Can they find any resonance with the world from which they have come, a relationship to that realm of the archetypes?

Music and Human Development

Music can be a powerful link to the world of the archetypes. In a lecture published in *The Inner Nature of Music and the Experience of Tone* Rudolf Steiner tells us that "the [young] child essentially dwells in moods of fifths."[4] The healthy young child lives in a state of consciousness which mirrors a much earlier stage of humanity's development. This stage is embodied in the music of the mood of the fifth, which brings a "breathing" experience between the spiritual and earthly worlds, a coexistence of these two states of being.

In prior stages of development, human beings had lived within the intervals of the seventh and then the sixth, which were solely experiences of the spiritual world—experiences of intuition and inspiration in which they lived outside of themselves. The stage of development in which they lived within the interval of the fifth occurred as humanity first began to experience an inner life, while still having a living experience of the spiritual world. This stage of development brought experiences of imagination.

"The interval of fifth is a real experience of imagination,"[5] Steiner says. Imagination is a spiritual experience, allowing the young child to breathe in the archetypal pictures of the spiritual world. These pictures imprint on the physical body and nourish the bodily-religious state of the child, bringing a pure bodily experience of gratitude into the organ-forming work within the physical body. The experience of the fifth, even in small doses, provides a deeply nourishing blessing to the young child's development.

Later developmental stages brought the experience of the fourth and third intervals. An experience of the spiritual world was no longer as strongly felt by the human being. Experiences of the major and minor third made it possible for human beings to have a sense of themselves, of inner self-awareness and emotional experience.[6] This experience of self-awareness has continued into the present, and is very appropriate for children age nine and older, as well as for adults. This experience of major and minor is not, however, recommended for younger children, especially those under age seven years, as it is more awakening and can contribute to "self-limitation," that sense of coming to know oneself within one's feelings.[7]

The Healing Nature of Mood-of-the-Fifth Music

The music of the mood of the fifth provides an essential bridge for the young child between the earthly and the spiritual worlds, helping to engender a feeling of being at home in both. Steiner states, "The experience of the fifth brings awareness of man within the divine world order. The experience of the fifth is, as it were, an expansion into the vast universe . . . he has forgotten his own self in the experience of the fifth in order to be among the gods . . ." [8] Through the experience of the fifth, human beings could feel that they stood within the spiritual world. This was such an important point that Steiner emphasizes that "the child should comprehend only fifths during the first years of school." [9] This does not mean that other music should not be brought to young children; it means to emphasize the importance of the experience of the fifth.

Perhaps even more today than in Steiner's time, with the increase of so many detrimental forces in society and the environment, experiencing the mood of the fifth can be very healing, helping young children to remain in dream-consciousness which fosters the healthy development of the physical body. The interval of the fifth helps to connect the young human being to the archetypal world, while allowing age-appropriate inner experiences of imagination and wonder at the world which is the child's earthly home.

In the kindergarten, my preference is to tune my instrument (kinderharp or lyre) to the frequency of A432 (rather than the more common A440). The slightly slower and deeper A432 positively affects the breath and heartbeat. In the kindergarten, my experience of playing and singing in the mood of the fifth has been that the children become more at ease and more imitative. I have found that this is an important way to help many of today's "awake" children find their way back into dream-consciousness.

Heiner Ruland writes of the role of the fifth in beginning to bridge the earthly and heavenly, and the outer and inner, worlds for the young child: "Thus, the fifth with its breath-like alternation between going out of oneself and drawing into oneself, is the earliest interval of musical self-discovery." He further states, "the fifth makes us feel we are at home in an earthly frame for the first time. Although the fifth always has the feeling of wide spaces—like a broad arching sky—still it is here that we first breathe the air of the earth and stand on firm ground. Its simple numerical relationship gives the interval something extraordinarily logical and conclusive . . .

downright geometrical. The ascending fifth . . . is like the question of a child, completely open to the world in its astonishment, selflessness, wonder and trust. It voices a question asked in complete assurance of an answer. A falling fifth . . . is the answer, an answer which states no opinions, but rather issues so out of the matter itself that it resolves all doubts."[10]

The mood of the fifth provides both experiences—question and answer—as it centers on the central tone of a′ (the sun/heart tone[11]), alternating between the ascending and descending fifths on either side (a′–e″–a′–d′–a′). The remaining notes—g′ and b′—of the pentatonic scale d′–e′–g′–a′–b′–d″–e″ may also be used in a balance around the a′, for example a′–b′–g′–a′, beginning and ending with a′. We hold back the tones c′ and f′, as well as half steps, until the more awakened age of nine and above.

A very important consideration in the use of the mood of the fifth is that it always allows the young child to have an objective, open experience, free from the subjectivity of the major and minor scales. In order to develop in healthy dream- consciousness, young children need to be left in objective freedom—free from the influences of both the major tonality, with its imposed brightness, and that of the minor, with its imposed darkness. These polar experiences are appropriate for age nine and above, when the child is awakening to conscious selfhood.

The Adult and the Mood of the Fifth

Developing a relationship to the mood of the fifth can be difficult for adults. Adults can feel a kind of emptiness in the fifth. As Steiner explains, "Naturally, man must experience something empty in the fifth, since he no longer has imaginations, and the fifth corresponds to an imagination, while the third corresponds to a perception within man's being. Today, therefore, man feels an emptiness in the fifth and must fill it with the substantiality of the instrument. This is the transition of the musical element from the more spiritual age to the later materialistic age."[12]

A question that I have lived with is, "Can the experience of the fifth become an invitation for the adult to re-awaken a sense of wonder, and imaginations of the spiritual world?" As an adult, it requires discipline to cultivate a true capacity for spiritual imagination. In the book *How to Know Higher Worlds*, Rudolf Steiner gives important exercises for the adult who is striving to consciously regain this capacity, which was naturally but unconsciously present in early childhood.

I have found that the interval of the fifth helps to gradually develop objectivity and openness to the world of sense perception and, further, to the imagination of what stands behind the sense-perceptible world. Within the fifth, there can be an experience of order and truth, which Heiner Ruland describes by saying, "The world of the fifth is musical geometry."[13]

Raising our own consciousness about the mood of the fifth allows us to develop our own relationship to it, as we share the blessing of music with young children.

Notes

1. Rudolf Steiner, *The Kingdom of Childhood,* (Hudson, NY: Anthroposophic Press, 1995), p. 18.

2. Audrey E. McAllen, "Birth to Seven Years," in Mary Ellen Willby, ed., *Learning Difficulties - A Guide for Teachers* (Fair Oaks, CA: Rudolf Steiner College Press, 1998), p. 245.

3. Rudolf Steiner, *The Child's Changing Consciousness as the Basis of Pedagogical Practice* (Hudson, NY: Anthroposophic Press, 1996), Lecture 8, p. 184.

4. Rudolf Steiner, *The Inner Nature of Music and the Experience of Tone* (Hudson, NY: Anthroposophic Press, 1983), Lecture 5, p. 58.

5. Steiner, *The Inner Nature of Music,* Lecture 6, p. 72.

6. Ibid., pp. 58, 72.

7. Wilma Ellersiek, "Mood of the Fifth With Central Tone A," in *Gesture Games for Spring and Summer* (Spring Valley, NY: Waldorf Early Childhood Association of North America, 2005), p. 14.

8. Steiner, *The Inner Nature of Music,* Lecture 6, p. 61.

9. Ibid., p. 66.

10. Heiner Ruland, *Expanding Tonal Awareness,* (Sussex, England: Rudolf Steiner Press, 1992), pp. 57, 75.

11. Rudolf Steiner gave a lecture on March 17, 1908 titled "Erden und Menschheitsentwicklung," ("Earthly and Human Development," not available in English). In this lecture Steiner mentioned the relationship between the seven metals and seven planets, and in a discussion session following the lecture, he proceeded to say there was a similar relationship between these and the seven tones. A translation of his statement follows: "The tones of music are related to the different metals in the following way: c–Iron–Mars; d–Quicksilver–Mercury; e–Tin–Jupiter; f–Copper–Venus; g–Lead–Saturn; a–Gold–Sun; b–Silver–Moon." The discussion was published in a newsletter (*Nachrichtenblatt der Rudolf Steiner Nachlassverwaltung, #26, 1969*) which can be viewed at http://bdn-steiner.ru/modules.php?name=H. In Maria Renold's book *Intervals, Scales, Tones and the Concert Pitch C=128 Hz* (Forest Row, UK: Temple Lodge, 2004) this discussion is also cited, with a chart on page 81 that shows the relationships.

    For the relationship between the sun and the human heart, see, for example, Rudolf Steiner, *Man: Hieroglyph of the Universe* (London: Rudolf Steiner Press, 1972), Lecture 3, page 46: "We only learn the significance of certain connections which we read from the stars, when we understand the corresponding processes in our organism; for what lies within our skin is no other than a reflection of the organism of the outer world. Thus if we draw a man in diagram, we have here the blood circulation (in diagram only) and we can trace its path. It is all in the inner being of Man. If we now go out into the Universe and look for the Sun, it is the Sun which corresponds to the heart within Man. What goes out from the heart through the body, or in point of fact out from the body to the heart, does in truth approximately resemble the movements connected with the course of the Sun."

12. Steiner, *The Inner Nature of Music,* Lecture 6, p. 63-64.

13. Ruland, p. 76.

Lisa Gromicko teaches kindergarten at Shining Mountain Waldorf School in Boulder, Colorado. For many years she has loved this work, especially the joy of sharing music with young children. She enjoys singing and regularly plays her soprano lyre. She has two grown sons, and with her husband is building an off-grid cabin in the Rocky Mountains.

The Mystery of the Mood of the Fifth

ANDREA LYMAN

As an experienced music educator, Andrea addresses the nature of the young child's experience of the world and of music as described by Rudolf Steiner, and helps us to understand the distinction between pentatonic music and music in the mood of the fifth.

What is this mysterious thing called *mood of the fifth*? How is it related to the pentatonic scale? Is it the same thing? Why would we choose to use it with the younger child, and what stands behind it pedagogically?

These questions arise repeatedly among Waldorf kindergarten teachers, class teachers, music teachers, students in teacher training centers, and those who choose to homeschool their children. In fact, I find that the mood of the fifth, which diverges so widely from the more familiar mainstream approach to music education, is the most misunderstood aspect of Waldorf music education. Although the concept of the mood of the fifth actually arises out of very specific indications given by Rudolf Steiner, it can be difficult to find much written about it.

The very nature and experience of mood of the fifth is something that lives naturally in the truth and reality of the young child, but no longer lives in the same way for the adult. Adults can find it challenging to understand and appreciate, because we can no longer *be* young children, and can no longer experience things *as* young children do. So, we must turn to study and research, and discover what Rudolf Steiner has to say about the young child's developmental stage of consciousness. Then we can enrich this study with our own experiences in bringing music to young children.

As in all of the Waldorf curriculum, we strive to meet the children at their particular stage of development in the most appropriate and soul-nurturing way, guided by our understanding of the importance of this developmental approach. This holds true for every aspect of early childhood work, and, with older children, for every subject, both in main lesson and in the special subjects, including music.

Steiner was quite clear about how the young child perceives the world, in light of the fact that the microcosmic earthly life of the individual human being mirrors the macrocosmic evolution of human consciousness. In describing the consciousness of the human being in the early post-Atlantean epochs, which correspond to the young child's consciousness, he says:

> *Man began to find the experience of the fifth more pleasant, and for a long time a scale composed according to our standards would have consisted of d, e, g, a, b, and again d and e. There was no f and no c. For the early post-Atlantean epochs, the feeling for f and c is missing; instead, the fifths throughout the tonal range of different octaves were experienced.*[1]

This statement mentions the interval of the fifth, two tones that are five tones apart (for example, d′ to a′, or e′ to b′), and enumerates the tones that made up the larger sequence of fifths spanning several octaves. Today, we transpose the tones and place them within the range of a ninth, or an octave plus one (for example, *d–e′–g′–a′–b′–d″–e″*), bringing them into our vocal range. This interval of a ninth reaches beyond the boundaries of the eight tones in the octave which reflects the musical boundaries of the consciousness of the healthy contemporary adult. However, it mirrors the expansiveness of the young child's experiences, in that she is not yet limited to the narrower earthly realm, but is very much still quite connected to, and living in, the spiritual world.

This gives us an indication of the tones to be used for the young child. These tones—d′–e′–g′–a′–b′—make up a pentatonic scale (*penta* means "five" and *tonic* "tone"), and comprise the scale or *set* of tones most appropriately brought to the younger child. It is also the scale that "lives" in the Choroi pentatonic children's lyres (kinderharps) and in the pentatonic flutes that we use in the lower school with the pre-nine-year old students. There are other pentatonic (five-tone) scales, but Steiner specifies this particular one, with the tone a′ at its center, for use in Waldorf education.

Many songs, such as folk songs of many cultures, use this pentatonic scale in various combinations and patterns. Some songs end on the tone g′ and have a major-sounding tonality. This tonality generally has an uplifting, happy, and bright quality. Pentatonic songs ending on the tone e′ have a more inner, contemplative, and darker quality, with a minor-sounding tonality. While not true diatonic major or minor scales (which include half steps), the "major" and "minor" pentatonic songs bring a subjective quality that Steiner states is more appropriate for the older child. Some pentatonic songs end on a b′, d′, or d″, and have a lovely unfinished feeling to them. These could be termed "neutral" pentatonic songs. All of these, however, are not necessarily in the mood of the fifth. Just as all squares are rectangles, but not all rectangles are squares, all mood-of-the-fifth songs can be said to be pentatonic, working within the parameters of that particular scale, but ***not all pentatonic songs are in the mood of the fifth***. And this is where much of the confusion may lie.

If we draw the notes of this pentatonic scale on a musical staff, we can see that there is a central tone, a tone that lies exactly in the center of the two outermost tones of e″ and d′. That tone is a′, and working with this a′ as a central tone, rather than working with a scale of ascending or descending steps, is a primary characteristic of music in the mood of the fifth.

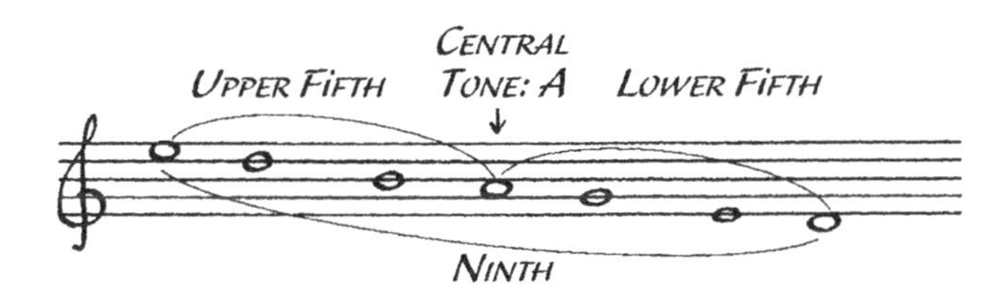

Rudolf Steiner describes the tones and their relationship with the various planets, sun, and moon. He tells us that the tone a′ corresponds to the sun,[2] the central light of our earthly experience and the realm out of which came the Christ Being. We could also say that this quality resides in our own human heart, the home of the Christ Being within us. It is our own *center*. The balanced form of mood of the fifth music, centered on the a′, serves the young child, who has newly descended from the spiritual world into the physical world, by helping orient him in himself and in the world.

From this central a′, we can weave our way up or down using the interval of a fifth (up to e″ or down to d′), starting and ending on this same central a′. However, the mood of the fifth is more than just singing fifths up or down from a′. While it is true that many of the songs include these intervals of fifths, the *quality* of this open, spirit-filled interval of a fifth can permeate a song even if a′ is the only tone used! And the other tones of the pentatonic scale can be used, of course, weaving around the a′, as the melodies eventually become more complex. It is called the *mood* of the fifth, not the *scale* of the fifth. It is truly about the mood that is carried by the melody, whether it is on one tone (a′) or several from this pentatonic scale. One could accurately say that mood of the fifth is really a *mood of soul*. Every aspect of how we *are* with the children creates this quality. It has an open-ended, unfinished character, and it is gentle and seemingly unstructured.

Another primary characteristic of mood of the fifth is an unmetered, free-flowing rhythmical melody. The words themselves create the rhythm; the rhythm is not tied to beat. These songs may not indicate a time signature or other measured notation, but may simply be intended to be sung with long and short note durations determined by how one might speak the words in sentences.

Essentially, rhythm groupings are in sets either of twos or threes. All meters and time signatures are made up of these two groupings. The archetype of three is associated with divinity (as in the Trinity). The archetype of two is associated with the human being, with its reality of polarity: consider the pairs in our own physiology! When used in music, these two different metric qualities can be experienced as flowing, dreamy, and more mobile (threes), or more structured, grounded, and awake (twos). In mood of the fifth, alternating between the feeling of these two patterns in a song can bring a looser structural quality, moving between wakefulness and dreaminess.

While most children are naturally rhythmic, it is better to wait until later to consciously introduce strong rhythm tied to beat, such as clapping, drumming, or marching to the beat of a song.

The child will comprehend a certain inner rhythm while it is still very young. Aside from this instinctively experienced rhythm, however, the child should not be troubled until after it is nine years old with the rhythm that is experienced, for example, in the elements of instrumental music. Only then should the child's attention be called to these things.[3]

Reading various descriptions of the mood of the fifth does not give a full understanding of it, since it is so *experiential*. There are, however, several hallmarks and qualities of the mood of the fifth that distinguish it from any other scale, mode, or tonality. Some of these important elements characterizing mood of the fifth are summarized as follows:

- The mood of the fifth is based on the d′-pentatonic scale, with the tone a′ at its center. This creates a mirrored scale (the tones create intervals that are mirrored on either side of the central tone a′). The melodies are simple, and do not necessarily use all the tones of the pentatonic scale.
- Songs usually begin and end on the tone a′.
- The intervals of a fifth, created by ascending from the a′ up to e″ and descending from the a′ down to d′, are most commonly used, often with the addition of smaller intervals balanced around the a′. However, a very simple mood-of-the-fifth song could even possibly use just one tone, the central a′.
- Songs in the mood of the fifth may be written with no meter, time signature, or strongly discernible underlying pulse or beat.
- There is a natural in- and out-breathing quality to the songs, both in melody and words. This quality meets the child's own still-developing physical breathing system, as well as strengthening healthy soul breathing.
- Characteristic of the mood of the fifth is an unfinished, open quality that does not bring the fully-incarnated or "landed" experience for the child; this will develop later around the nine-year change.
- Overall, the mood of the fifth is just that: a *mood*, one that carries a quality of being that is gentle, reverent, and respectful of the children at their stage of development, bringing them what is soul-nurturing.

In Waldorf education, we work from the whole to the parts. Young children experience life holistically. If we wish them to experience music as a whole, then, we will realize that analysis, theory, and the separating out of the musical elements of melody, rhythm, and harmony do not have a rightful place in what we bring to them. Mood of the fifth music is complete for the young child and contains the entire cosmos within it. The child feels at one with the world: that he *is* the world, and the world is *he*. In explaining the consciousness of the epoch which a child under the age of nine recapitulates, Steiner says the following:

Such music made a person feel as if he were carried into a different element. In the music of the fifths [Quintenmusik], a human being felt lifted out of himself . . . Formerly, when he experienced fifths, he would have been inclined to say, 'The angel in my being is beginning to play music. The muse in me speaks.' 'I sing' was not the appropriate expression . . . [4]

For young children, we must provide the musical experiences necessary to allow them to stay connected to this world from which they have recently descended. When we bring them down into their material incarnation too soon, it brings a hardening effect; we wake them up too soon, and deprive them of the soul nourishment they need at this time to develop in a healthy way. Steiner reminds us what is most musically appropriate for the child under nine years of age:

All this is extraordinarily important when one is faced with the task of guiding the evolution of the human being regarding the musical element. You see, up to about the age of nine, the child does not possess a proper grasp of major and minor moods . . . Though it is not readily admitted, the child essentially dwells in moods of fifths. Naturally, one can resort in school to examples already containing thirds, but if one really wishes to reach the child, musical appreciation must be based on the appreciation of fifths; this is what is important. One does the child a great kindness if one confronts it with major and minor music moods as well as an appreciation for the whole third-complex sometime after the age of nine . . . [5]

Creating an atmosphere of openness, imagination, and gentleness in our gestures, with our voices, and in the very way we handle instruments and materials, greatly contributes to the mood of the fifth. Physical gestures and movement done smoothly and gently can accompany the singing, and can be used to portray the story or content of the song. Moving in a circle (both around, and in and out), dancing freely, and creating large, whole-body movements are all health-giving for the etheric forces. Singing, while using lovely large silks wafting naturally up and down, can bring a beautiful quality of soul-breathing, which is so important as we work with young children. They love to lift up the silks and then allow them to float downward.

The experience of the fifth arose, and during this time man still felt united with what lived in his breath. He said to himself—though he did not say it, he felt it . . .—"I breathe in, I breathe out . . . . The musical element, however, does not live in me at all; it lives in inhalation and exhalation. Man felt always as if he were leaving and returning to himself in the musical experience. The fifth comprised both inhalation and exhalation . . . [6]

When I taught music in the public schools before coming to Waldorf education over twenty-one years ago, I was required to teach according to the curriculum mandated by the school districts in which I taught. Although this took place in two different states, the approach to what should be taught, and when, was quite similar. A high value was placed on encouraging children to read traditional notation as soon as possible. Even as early as kindergarten, there was emphasis on teaching theory, history, performance, and repertoire, as well as reading traditional notation. These young children, while eager to sing and engage in music making, were being asked to enter into a realm that was quite dead for them. It had nothing to do with their *experience* of music, with listening, with creating, with truly living *in* the music itself.

The color drained from their faces, they became restless, and eventually they lost their natural enthusiasm. Rudolf Steiner gives us a very different picture of what we must bring to the young child:

> *. . . [G]ive the children lessons in music right from the very beginning, and at first, as far as possible to accustom them to sing little songs, quite empirically without any kind of theory: nothing more than simply singing little songs, but they must be well sung! . . . [F]irst you must accustom the children to sing little songs as a whole . . .* [7]

It is important to remember that when we are singing with the children, we must use a light, free voice, singing songs using these pentatonic tones, and not descending below c′ (middle C). This is a higher range than what many of us may be used to singing, and certainly higher than the range in which most adults speak. We must learn to lift up our voices to meet the tone quality and natural range of the young child's voice, so that the children can emulate us in a healthy way. Contributing to the true nature of mood of the fifth is the healthy vocal practice of using this higher, light, free voice when singing. However, this does not imply that we should not use our own natural voice. For male voices, this means singing in their *natural* range, but doing so with a quality that is light and genuine. If males sing in their falsetto voice (that is, sing an octave higher to match the pitch of the children's voices), the children will try to imitate this and will also try to sing an octave higher. It is also important to consistently find the starting pitch before singing, and to begin each song on the same pitch each time. This develops excellent intonation skills both in ourselves and in the children, and cultivates deep listening—a skill we must reclaim in our human experience.

Using a whole-body gesture system (it can be called a "body script") can bring an experience of the relationship between the tones and the physical body. This "body script" cultivates our sense of pitch, and can occasionally be done with the children as well—though of course never speaking about it, simply carrying out the movements while singing a song. The children may follow along with their imitative movements, but we do not call any attention to it. The tone a′ is indicated with both hands crossed at the heart, for it truly is the center, the sun tone. The interval of an ascending fifth (from a′ up to e″) is shown with arms outstretched above the head with palms facing heavenward. This tone, e″, goes beyond the boundary of the octave (d′ to d″), and represents the still-strong connection of the young child with the spiritual world. Moving downward a fifth from a′ to d′, we bend down to touch our feet, not the floor; this will come later, when middle C (c′) is introduced after the nine-year change, when the child has landed more firmly on the earth. Moving in this way, singing the tones a′ to e″, and a′ to d′, in a weaving lemniscate, always returning to the a′ in the middle, allows us to hear, feel, and move the fifths easily. We can gradually add the g′ and b′ on either side of the a′ and continue this floating movement around a′.

These five tones can be used exclusively for a very long time to great delight and satisfaction of the children. A distinctive quality of mood-of-the-fifth music is its simplicity. The best songs for young children are those with an extremely simple melody, ones that use the fifths, starting and ending on, as well as weaving around, the central a′. The very simplest of all would be a little song on just one single tone. If sung truly in a reverent mood, a song using only the tone a′ for the entire song can be deeply gratifying and meaningful for the young child.

Working with the pentatonic children's lyre can be another important way to deepen our own, as well as the children's, experience of the mood of the fifth. The lyre's timbre and purity of tone lend themselves to the deep listening that is required to experience the spiritual realities of tone, and we can sound the interval of the fifth in a way that mirrors the singing. The young child hears peripherally, and this instrument brings the kind of sounding that nourishes this capacity, as it creates a tonal atmosphere surrounding the child.

To many adults, mood-of-the-fifth music can be very unsatisfying because our more evolved consciousness wants to hear stronger finality at the end of a song, a landing place that is inwardly pleasing to our adult ears. I have met many teachers who speak about their own boredom with, or even dislike of, the mood of the fifth. And it is right that we, as adults, should not find it musically satisfying for ourselves, because it lives totally outside the way we have grown into our own hearing and musical perception, as well as our distance from what we experienced and perceived *as* children. Rudolf Steiner sheds light on the adult's discomfort with the mood of the fifth when he says,

> *The experience of the fifth as spiritual experience was the first to be lost to humanity. Modern man does not have the experience of the fifth that still existed, let us say, four to five hundred years before our era. At that time the human being truly felt in the experience of the fifth, 'I stand within the spiritual world.' He required no instrument in order to produce outwardly the interval of a fifth. Because he still possessed imaginative consciousness, he felt that the fifth, which he himself had produced, took its course in the divine realm."* [8]

The young child, however, completely lives *in* this mood, with these fifths, with the unfinished, open quality of mood of the fifth music, because it mirrors exactly where she is developmentally. We are not bringing these particular musical experiences for ourselves, but rather for the appropriate developmental needs of the children, to meet them where they are, giving them "soul food." Steiner has indicated that before the nine-year change, we bring the music to the child, and after the nine-year change, we ask the child to meet the music.

In my work with young children, I see them respond most favorably to that which feeds their souls. They do not tire of simple, gentle, and deliberate mood-of-the-fifth music. It satisfies them inwardly, and allows them the opportunity to live fully in their still-strong connection to the spiritual world. In the interval of the fifth itself, the young child can feel himself a part of the spiritual world. When children are not feeling met, a nervous tension begins to encroach, and chaotic or disruptive behavior will frequently result. When they are given what truly meets them at a soul level, there is an ease, and a feeling of being genuinely cared for. This is the mystery of the mood of the fifth.

Notes

1. Rudolf Steiner, *The Inner Nature of Music and the Experience of Tone* (Hudson, NY: Anthroposophic Press, 1983), Lecture V, p. 51.

2. Rudolf Steiner gave a lecture on March 17, 1908 titled "Erden und Menschheitsentwicklung," ("Earthly and Human Development," not available in English). In this lecture, Steiner mentioned the relationship between the seven metals and seven planets, and in a discussion session following the lecture, he proceeded to say there was a similar relationship between these and the seven tones. A translation of his statement follows: "The tones of music are related to the different metals in the following way: c–Iron–Mars; d–Quicksilver–Mercury; e–Tin–Jupiter; f–Copper–Venus; g–Lead–Saturn; a–Gold–Sun; h–Silver–Moon." The discussion was published in a newsletter (*Nachrichtenblatt der Rudolf Steiner Nachlassverwaltung*, #26, 1969) which can be viewed at http://bdn-steiner.ru/modules.php?name=H. In Maria Renold's book *Intervals, Scales, Tones and the Concert Pitch C=128 Hz* (Forest Row, UK: Temple Lodge, 2004) this discussion is also cited; there is a chart on page 81 that shows the relationships.

3. Steiner, *The Inner Nature of Music*, p. 67.

4. Ibid., pp. 51-52.

5. Ibid., pp. 57-58.

6. Ibid., pp. 55-56.

7. Rudolf Steiner, *The Kingdom of Childhood* (London: Rudolf Steiner Press, 1974), p. 112.

8. Steiner, *The Inner Nature of Music*, Lecture VI, p. 62.

Andrea Lyman holds Bachelor's and Master's degrees in vocal music education, and taught music in the public school setting (K-12) for many years before becoming a parent and happily finding Waldorf education in 1992. She has been teaching Waldorf music for twenty years and received her certification in Waldorf Music Education in 2005 from Sunbridge College. She has taught music courses through Sunbridge College, West Coast Institute, and Sound Circle Center. Her two-part article, "Let There Be Music: The Music Curriculum in the Waldorf School (Grades 1-8)" appeared in Renewal *Magazine in 2009. She is currently president of AWME (The Association for Waldorf Music Education) and organizes its annual Waldorf Music Conference each summer, as well as traveling as a music mentor to Waldorf schools throughout North America.*

Music, Mobility, and the Mood of the Fifth

SHEILA PHELPS JOHNS

The importance of balanced mobility in music for the young child is emphasized in this article, in which Sheila brings her years of experience as a teacher to a close look at the role of mirrored intervals in the mood of the fifth.

One of the fundamental principles that informs our work as Waldorf early childhood educators is an understanding of the evolution of human consciousness from childhood to adulthood. In my work with parents of young children, I have the privilege of using music as a medium through which it is particularly possible to experience this basic truth. We could well ask, "Is a young child's experience of music different from our adult experience of music? If so, is there a way for us to deepen our adult understanding of how the young child experiences music?"

As a premise, we could say that a young child's experience of *everything* is different from our own, particularly in the realm of sense experience. Indeed, Rudolf Steiner tells us that a little child is actually entirely sense organ.[1] The child's sense experience is both more expanded and more refined than that of an adult, and this is particularly true with the child's aural sense. For the young child, "hearing" is at once "being," and we could truly say that the child's whole being is music.

For the child, everything in his or her environment "sings," from the melodic lilt of the mother's speaking voice, to the rhythmic pounding of a hammer, to the harmony of a babbling brook. Considering the young child's experience, we would, in fact, need to expand the traditional definition of music altogether. If love is a verb, then surely music is an adverb! Music is actually a way of living. We can speak musically, think musically, and move musically.

Music implies mobility, which can be experienced particularly through the musical element of melody. Musical melody creates a "curved" gesture of movement, which stands in stark contrast to the high-tech, digital world around us that is characterized by ever more subtle variations on "straight." In a larger sense, we experience our humanness, and thus our musicality, in the mobility of our breathing, feeling, singing, and dancing, which, taken together, define the natural state of the healthy child.

In *The Development of the Human Senses,* Willi Aeppli states: "The young child hears music . . . less with the ear than with his whole body, which vibrates and lives in the musical element. His whole physical being is either in harmony or disharmony."[2] Harmony can be understood as a state of balance that is the basis of a healthy childhood. For the first seven years, the young child's consciousness is still united with the world around him. The child's whole life experience consists in reaching out into the world and then gathering the totality of his experience back into himself, which is a gesture of movement from the center out to the periphery and back again—the fundamental movement of the breath.

If the child's whole being is music, we should expect to be able to find such a breathing movement in a specific musical form that reflects this underlying gesture of childhood. And we do indeed find exactly that potential in the sequence of tones Rudolf Steiner indicated as archetypal for the young child: d′ e′ g′ a′ b′, and then again, d″ e″—the tones we use to create music in the mood of the fifth.[3]

In her book *Giving Love—Bringing Joy*, Wilma Ellersiek states: "Mood of the fifth with central tone a′ corresponds to the cosmic experience of the child in the first seven years, who is still at one with the world and does not yet feel a polarity between it and himself. This musical mode forms a protective shelter in which the child can feel secure. Mood of the fifth signifies unity with the cosmos, in which heavens and earth are yet united. It means being in harmony with a divine center."[4]

How is this so? Starting from the "Sun Tone," as Rudolf Steiner refers to the central a′,[5] three pairs of tones ray out in exact mirrored distances on either side of that center, in the following fashion: d′ e′—g′ **a′** b′—d′ e″.

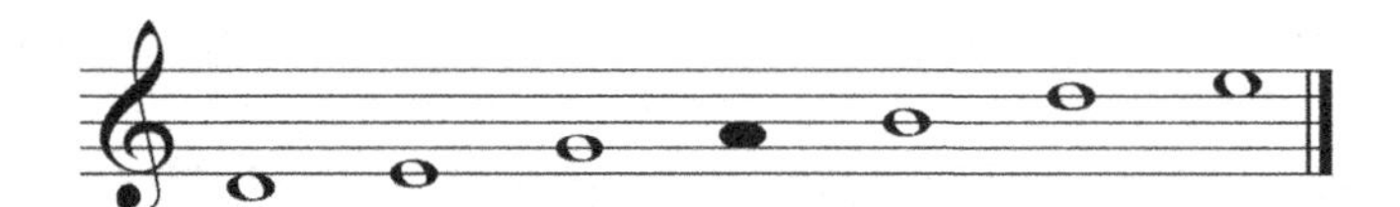

The outermost d′ and e″ lie five tones from the center in each direction, creating the interval of a fifth on either side—an interval that Ellersiek calls "a tonal space of optimal balance" for the young child. Looked at *in sequence*, the distance between the low d′ and the high e″ actually creates the interval distance of a ninth.

Looked at *in movement* around the central a′, however, we experience a double fifth in a perfect mirror around the central tone.

Used in sequence, the seven tones named above are certainly one expression of the archetypal five-tone pentatonic scale. What sets them apart as an expression of music in the mood of the fifth is how they can be *moved* as mirrored intervals around the central tone a′.

Any odd-numbered interval (a third or a seventh, for example) contains within it a central tone with a mirrored interval on either side. For example, the interval of the third g′—b′ contains a central tone a′ with an interval of a second on either side. The mirrored seconds can be heard melodically by sounding, for example, **a′** b′ **a′** g′ **a′**; or, **a′** g′ **a′** b′ **a′**.

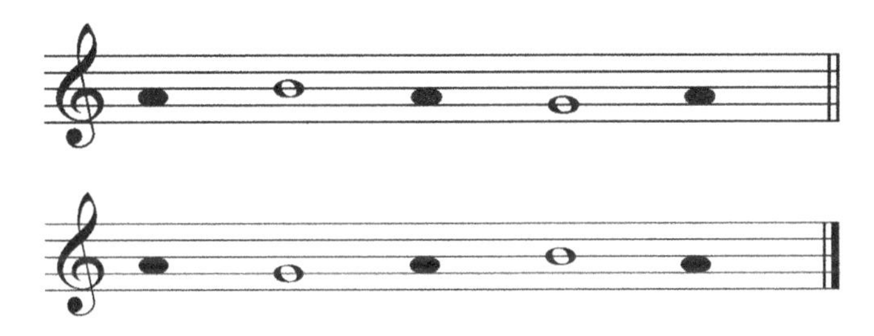

Again with a′ at the center, we can hear mirrored fourths: **a′** d″ **a′** e′ **a′**; or, **a′** e′ **a′** d″ **a′**;

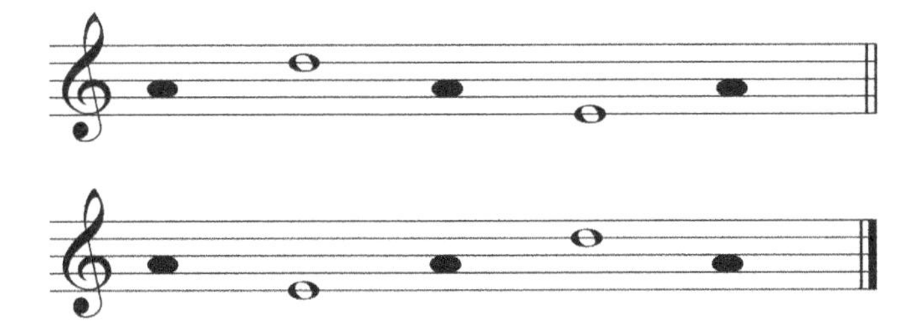

and mirrored fifths: **a′** e″ **a′** d′ **a′**; or, **a′** d′ **a′** e″ **a′**.

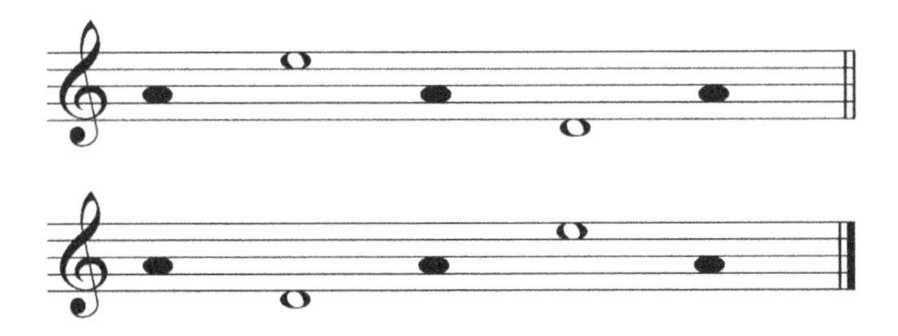

Though it is certainly possible to bring any interval into a mirrored movement, there is something special about the mirrored fifth in this sequence of tones, as it is the only odd-numbered interval of the three pairs that weave around the central tone "A". Because a fifth, in its form, is balanced within itself, when this interval is created both above and below a central tone, creating the span of a double fifth, we may get a glimpse into the mystery of what Ellersiek may have meant in her reference to this "tonal space of optimal balance."

These mirrored forms could be drawn with a continuous stroke, resulting in a form reminiscent of the infinity symbol, referred to by Rudolf Steiner as the lemniscate. In drawing this form, illustrated here with the interval of a fifth, we experience an archetypal movement of balance, just as hearing the tones brings a sense of balanced movement around a central tone.

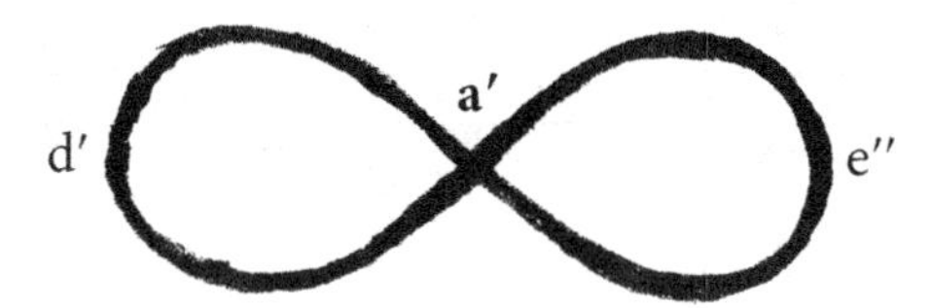

Rudolf Steiner has brought us the insight that each human being recapitulates in his own developing consciousness the stages of evolving consciousness of all of humanity. In fact, the sequential unfolding of the entire Waldorf curriculum through the grades is based on this very premise.

If we look at the history of music (or any of the arts), we can actually see that it reveals a picture of the human being's developing consciousness, in which we have progressed over time from an expanded to a more contracted state of consciousness. From the point of view of musical intervals, Steiner points out that in times of pre-history, the more cosmic consciousness of the human being caused him to find the very large intervals of the ninth and, somewhat later, the seventh to be the most pleasing. Coming into the earliest eons of recorded history, the evolving human being began to prefer the interval of the fifth, and this then became the most centrally important interval of music right into the eleventh century. Developmentally, we could identify the young child with this very period of history, in which physical activity, imaginative consciousness, and sense experience formed the basis of "knowing." In our pedagogy, we seek to surround young children with these very kinds of affirmations of their particular stage of development, and it follows, therefore, that we would wish to do the same thing with the music that we bring to them.

The gesture of mirroring invites mobility, an experience affirming that which is most essentially human in us. This concept can be a real gift in working with parents who may have lost their own confidence and comfort with singing. To begin with, the simple use of the three central tones g′ a′ b′, when moved freely around the a′, can provide the basis for a simple improvised tune that is infinitely appropriate and organic for the child, and well within the grasp of any adult. Julius Knierim, in his foundational book on music in the mood of the fifth,[6] observes the following: "What healthy children reveal of 'hidden' music through their movements can, together with what they sing, lead the adult who has remained inwardly flexible and 'mobile' to an understanding of how the young child experiences music."

When the mirrored seven-tone pentatonic scale with central tone a′ is contrasted with the sequential eight-tone diatonic scale familiar in traditional Western music, we become aware of an even deeper implication. As Ellersiek points out, a diatonic scale has a different structure: There are two centers, in that a contrast is established between the fundamental tone and its octave. In this context, half-steps creating minor and major intervals give rise to minor and major modes. This duality of modes corresponds to the phenomenon of the duality of self with the world—of inner and outer—unlike the unity achieved through the mood of the fifth. Elleriek states, "In the songs for the first seven years of life, this duality should not yet be broached."

An enhanced experience of this mood of the fifth in music can be found through the use of the seven-string pentatonic lyre that contains the same tones of d′ e′ g′ a′ b′ d′ e″. Although a detailed look at the unsurpassed value of this instrument in our work with young children is regrettably beyond the scope of this article, a few things may nevertheless be observed here.

Beyond the sounding of pure tones that cultivates listening like almost no other instrument, accompanying our singing with the pentatonic lyre can support the voice and bring strength and objectivity to the sounding of the sung tones (particularly those in the upper register that are so natural for a child and so often challenging for an adult!). In addition, the layout of the strings on this instrument can provide any teacher who wishes to achieve a clear understanding of the mood of the fifth with a visual, physical representation of the movement around the central tone a′. We can right away *see* that the space created by "moving" each of the three pairs of intervals around the center is one of perfect balance.

I have long experienced the mood of the fifth as an archetypal picture of our threefold nature, with polarities around a center. This picture has become central in all of my work, as I believe that it reflects a much more all-encompassing universal truth that suggests the reality of The Middle Way—a marked contrast to the principal of duality we see musically reflected in the diatonic scale. In recent years, it has been verified that in addition to the scientific phenomena of the overtone series (the sequence of predictable intervals that arise inaudibly when a single tone is sounded), there also exists an undertone series (also referred to as a counter-series or complementary series)[7] which is even harder to detect, arising as an exact mirror on the *other* side of the sounded tone.

This principle can be further illustrated by the reflecting movement of the human being's etheric body of formative forces,[8] that body which is undergoing the most intensive development exactly during the first seven years of life.

Several months ago, one of my first grade lyre students gave me a priceless peek into the reality of the unity-consciousness of a young child. This seven-year-old had begun working with the lyre during his final spring in the kindergarten. One day he came into his lesson beaming, and proudly announced to me that he had figured out that the lyre has an "even" number of strings. (Clearly this was a new first grade concept with which he was working.) Puzzled at first, I chose not to contradict him, but rather asked him with interest to show me. He pulled out his lyre and proceeded to play the bottom d′ and the top e″. "Okay," he said, "here are two." Then he moved in one string further on each side, sounding the bottom e′ and the top d″. "Here are two more—that's four." Finally, he played the two on either side of the center, the g′ and the b′. "There!" he exclaimed, "Two, four, six—and six is an even number!" I paused before proceeding. "What about this one?" I finally asked, pointing to the a′. He immediately responded, "Oh, that one doesn't count because it's in the middle." He looked thoughtful for a minute and then went on, "You know, kind of like me." He suddenly put the lyre down, stood, and exclaimed, "I have two arms and two legs—and *I* am in the center!"

In his lecture of December 2, 1922, Rudolf Steiner states, "Song is an earthly means of recalling the experience of pre-earthly existence."[9] If song alone has this power, then giving a central place in our work to music in the mood of the fifth, during the time of development when the young child is recapitulating the stage of humanity that resonated most deeply with the interval of the fifth, can surely make this recalling even more potent—an experience of music in balanced movement that affirms to the child his unique place in the universe, illustrated since time immemorial in the sacred maxim, "As above, so below."

Notes

1. Rudolf Steiner, *The Spiritual Ground of Education*, lectures given in Oxford, Aug. 16-25, 1922 (London, 1947), p. 12

2. Willi Aeppli, *The Development of the Human Senses* (Forest Row, England: Rudolf Steiner Schools Fellowship, 2012).

3. Rudolf Steiner, *The Inner Nature of Music and the Experience of Tone,* Lecture of March 7, 1923 (Anthroposophic Press, 1983), p. 51

4. Wilma Ellersiek, *Giving Love—Bringing Joy: Hand Gesture Games and Lullabies in the Mood of the Fifth* (Spring Valley, NY: Waldorf Early Childhood Association of North America, 2003). See also the excerpt "Creating a Protective Tonal Space" on pages 11 to 16 of this volume.

5. Rudolf Steiner gave a lecture on March 17, 1908 titled "Erden und Menschheitsentwicklung," ("Earthly and Human Development," not available in English). In this lecture Steiner mentioned the relationship between the seven metals and seven planets, and in a discussion session following the lecture, he proceeded to say there was a similar relationship between these and the seven tones. A translation of his statement reads: "The tones of music are related to the different metals in the following way: c–Iron–Mars; d–Quicksilver–Mercury; e–

Tin–Jupiter; f–Copper–Venus; g–Lead–Saturn; a–Gold–Sun; b–Silver–Moon." The discussion was published in a newsletter (*Nachrichtenblatt der Rudolf Steiner Nachlassverwaltung*, #26, 1969) which can be viewed at http://bdn-steiner.ru/modules.php?name=H. In Maria Renold's book *Intervals, Scales, Tones and the Concert Pitch C* (Forest Row, UK: Temple Lodge, 2004) this discussion is also cited, with a chart on page 81 that shows the relationships.

6. Julius Knierim, *Quintenlieder: Music for Young Children in the Mood of the Fifth* (Fair Oaks, CA: Rudolf Steiner College Press, 1994).

7. Anny von Lange, *Man, Music, and Cosmos*, Volume I (Sussex, England: Rudolf Steiner Press, 1992), Chapter 3.

8. See, for example, Rudolf Steiner, *Anthroposophy: An Introduction* (Anthroposophical Publishing Company, 1961), Lecture 2, January 20, 1924, p. 34, in regard to the counter-image of a physical movement. See also Joep Eikenboom, *Foundations of the Extra Lesson* (Fair Oaks, CA: Rudolf Steiner College Press, 2007), Chapter 9, pp. 122-123, "Reflection in the Ether Body," which refers, among other things, to the Rudolf Steiner lectures "The Balance in the World and Man: Lucifer and Ahriman" (Dornach, Nov. 20-22, 1914).

9. Rudolf Steiner, *The Inner Nature of Music and the Experience of Tone*, p. 35.

Sheila Phelps Johns has worked with the lyre in the early grades at the Washington Waldorf School since 1998, where she is also a member of the Care Group. She has completed anthroposophic trainings in both vocal and instrumentally based music therapy. She works with music therapeutically at the school and through her private practice in Silver Spring, Maryland. Through her experience of working with music and the developing child, she has become an advocate and educator of music in early childhood.

The Music Curriculum through the Waldorf Approach

CHRISTOF-ANDREAS LINDENBERG

The following article is based on notes taken at Christof-Andreas Lindenberg's opening talk at the August, 1993 conference of the Lyre Association of North America, held in Harlemville, New York. In reading these notes, even when they are somewhat aphoristic, we can contemplate the musical approach to early childhood in the context of the full spectrum of the music curriculum.

The Lyre Association of North America chose the above theme for its annual conference at the request of many teachers eager to understand Rudolf Steiner's indications about the musical human being. In the first lecture of the cycle *Practical Advice to Teachers,* Rudolf Steiner says, "Man's nature, we shall find, is such that he is in a way a born musician . . . Man is born into the world in such a way that makes him want to join his own bodily nature in a musical rhythm and relationship with the world."[1] The growing child is not *like*, but *is*, a musical instrument, which becomes ever more finely tuned as the pre-birth music of the spheres manifests as melody, the ever-hummed tune that skips along, harmonizing in the rhythms of heartbeat and breath to arrive at the awakening beat of "I am an individual in the world." To accompany the incarnating child, the right musical "response" is needed.

Rudolf Steiner spoke of "true dawn hearing," the Michael call. This is a hearing that is not measured so much in quantity of decibels, but rather in the subtlety of after-tones and projected sound. One can be convinced that instruments like the Choroi flute and the lyre came down from heaven, down from the dawn of Michael-hearing, as it were, to aid us. It was Rudolf Steiner, in mentioning (in 1924) the need for a "kithara-like instrument," who planted a seed with Lothar Gärtner and Edmund Pracht for a new musical instrument, which they later developed into the lyre. If Rudolf Steiner could have known about the existence of such a new instrument, he probably would have advised us differently, and in more detail, about the child's music in the first years at school!

Early Childhood

Through Rudolf Steiner we learn that music and the incarnating child are one and the same. We have especially to experience the singing child as an instrument. The embryo, preparing for birth, has a shape that we could describe as that of an ear. The way in which the embryo perceives the mother's heartbeat determines the way the child will speak. Already as an embryo we are able to hear. In spiritual science we learn that the sense of hearing was developed even before the evolutionary stage of Old Saturn. In the first chapter of St. John's Gospel it is stated, "In the beginning was the Word." There must have been some presence, gifted with a *prime*-ordial sense of hearing, to perceive this word. One of Rudolf Steiner's first messages to the first Waldorf teachers was that *man is born musical*—he is a "born musician."

Rudolf Steiner describes this musical force as a will force, active in the creation of the world—active also in the child's body—a musical will. Thus there is a natural drive in a child to dance. It is good, therefore, to do eurythmy with three- to four-year-olds. We do not know what happens to a child who has sat and watched, as statistics for American preschool children show, *4000 hours of television*, when actually he or she should have danced!

The periphery of the body belongs to the musically-created world; hence, we do finger games, ring games, and dances with the preschool child. All of nature is a reflected form of the music of the spheres. The arrangements of flower petals have tonal forms, as also occur in the sounding forms of the Chladni figures, and these tonal forms are an active force in the child's body.

The preschool child moves from out of the periphery, through the legs and arms. Hence, we can use sounding matter—sticks, stones, and metals—without formal, directed applications in music-making. All of our senses also belong to the periphery, and are derived from these musical forces. Steiner speaks of the ear as being "musically attuned" and the eye as sensitive to "shapes and forms," both having derived from this inborn musical element within the child. As the child enters a process of emancipation from his sense experiences, a new step of self-consciousness dawns. This is when we play "Poor Jenny Sits A-Weeping," as the child is cast out from the circle of the ring game. When the children begin first grade, singing and playing of instruments become more formal.

The Mood of the Fifth through Second Grade

We must imagine that the astral body, embodying musical laws, works on the physical body; therefore, we have to play instruments as the musical extension of the body. A child must also sing. It is an up-building force, an etheric activity prompted by the astral body. From the fourth lecture of the supplementary course of June 1921, we learn that *listening* heals and harmonizes what comes about through the head organization working on the body, and—equally important—that *singing* heals what the body is meant to supply to the head.[2]

This riddlesome statement becomes verified in the practical doing. In kindergarten and first grade the children listen to melody around them as a force that works onto the body. At that age they are "held" by a certain heaven, a pre-birth melody element around them. The limbs shoot out towards the earthly ground; in fact, we can say the child grows down, not up! Musically, even the first and second grade child does not touch the ground yet at all.

In singing we work from the middle: A middle tone (a′) is the orientation, and we can place the tones, up to a fifth above and a fifth below, around it like a dance. The diagram that follows is only meant for the teacher's reference, of course.

Now the *mood of the fifth*, a sequence of tones centered around a′, becomes an experience which goes beyond what is normally termed a pentatonic scale. In such singing, the body, indeed, works "back onto the head." Thus, listening and singing are two different directions of working.

Rudolf Steiner even suggests dividing the class into two groups, a listening group and a singing group. (It is to be understood that these are meant to be *mutual* groups in the same room, which will naturally take turns.)

We need to come to a reduction of the tonal spectrum from two-and-a-half octaves down to the space of a double fifth—of the seven tones from d′ to e″—as a necessary hemming in, encompassing a scale of the mood of the fifth. This also means that we must take away all harmonization and chords, which so easily creep into our teaching when, as adults, we cannot imagine what children of that age really feel like. They are not looking for major or minor harmonies. The melody itself speaks a direct, unburdened, and fulfilled language.

Too much resonance in instruments stimulates hearing of the harmonies of the overtone series. Never forget how Steiner describes the child coming to school as too musical! Steiner, thereby, also implies the oversensitivity towards overtones. Edmund

Pracht did away with unnecessary embellishments of the piano when creating the idea of the lyre. What is too strong in the overtone structure makes the first grader faint in the end. Since the child is an instrument himself, you do well not to impose your big piano on him.

The other golden rules for the mood of the fifth are: Work mainly with descending melodies, centering on a′; and, if at all possible, work with un-harmonized songs and de-emphasized beat. Right hearing and real harkening adjusts the positioning of the larynx, so there should be moments when you sing and play to the children while they just sit still and listen.

All this holds good for the second grade as well, except that the songs get more rhythmical. The head, along with the melody of "heaven" around it, seems to grow smaller, and the arms and legs just itch to move. This is the time to play the Choroi flute! In second grade, with the second dentition taking effect, the child jumps up and down the space of the body. Within the space of the octave there are two "jumps": the interval of a fourth above the lower fifth, which is the space of the actual song—

—or the fourth up from the lowest note of the song, with the main body of song in the upper fifth space.

The second grader, in movement, seems to consist of two halves, as arms and legs get entangled in the action songs.

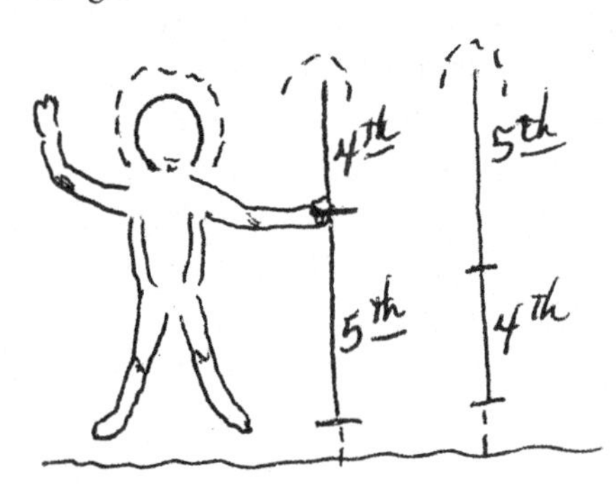

Third Grade

In third grade all the animals gather in the ark, and it comes to land on firm ground. The movement slows down a bit, drawings begin to show dark colors, and we prepare to build a house on firm foundations. We should build a house as big as the child who now feels *in* his body. Somehow the laws of that house are not merely reflected in the outer building of it; the effect is also a moral one. This is the time to come to the ground note c′, to introduce the ascending scale and melody triads: "the roof, the floor, the window, and the door."

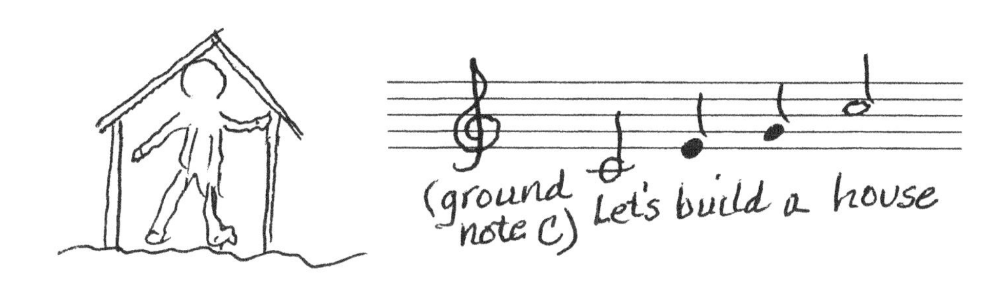

Music writing begins. The child of nine years and older now makes the step from the mood of the fifth and pentatonic songs to the diatonic scale and melodies which are well-grounded, beginning and ending on a tonic: farming and work songs, craft songs, and number songs. Up to this point in grade three we had to mold the music with special care; now we find each other on the same earth, with a common tonic note. Songs in unison, accompanied melodically with lyres and flutes, begin to have a different ring to them, a new meaning. Now it is possible to introduce a simple minor tune such as "Let Me of God a Fighter Be" (Künstler) or "Hey Do Ro Lot, My Bonny Bonny Boat."

Fourth Grade

As to fourth grde, Rudolf Steiner said that only now is there a beginning sentient element in the child. The fourth graders see each other quite differently than before: for the first time there are teams and groups; individuals are either more introverted or extroverted—minor or major. We sing alternating and echo songs, ostinatos and songs in parallel thirds, keeping the two-fold nature of the Dionysian and Apollonian approaches flexible in music. Between question and answer there is always an ascending and descending of tones, and it is now necessary to work in groups facing each other. The first term can cover much of this, leading to the *round*, when the child discovers that everybody is moving simultaneously in equal steps but using different parts of the melody—and lo! Harmony begins to arise.

What is *new* is to be able to play a chord on a Bordun lyre, with whole groups of them playing two or three chords alternately. On the recorder/flute, b-flat and f-sharp are introduced and other instruments come in. Small ensembles now accompany the singing. Harmony is achieved in many steps, mainly joining two melodies—alternating, echoing, supplementing, and in parallel. Chords play a secondary role in this first approach.

The crowning of this part of the way is the round, which should not have come before fourth grade. Now the gateway for major and minor—music's most powerful expression—can be passed through. *Major* stands for what in us is "the king of the castle—ha, hey, ho—and you are the poorest rascal," and *minor,* for when we feel that the world is bigger than us.

One could either use strong or so-called weak minor songs to touch upon what might be felt in the now-developing *sentient soul element* of children. "Three Gypsies Stood at the Castle Gate" is a defiant, strong minor, while "Little Red Bird of the Lonely Moor" is a song evoking compassion for the vulnerable subject. Just as in fourth grade a feeling of fairness develops in the preparedness for sport, so in music, a feeling of respect for the other "team" or person awakens. There should be a lot of two-part singing with exchanging of parts, a dependence on musical teams.

Fifth Grade

In fifth grade we explore the Greek culture, with a refined feeling for active and passive moods—which corresponds in music to a change of key signature, effecting a different level or mood. Rules of how to behave among the people (*polis* in Greek) are also experienced in the rules of music! We can bring the Greek modes for the different regions of Greece, as an experience of a differentiated musical geography among one people.

The new musical form is the "catch." Can you jump on the bandwagon at the right moment? As the right posture is exercised in the pentathlon—the five Greek exercises of running, jumping, wrestling, discus, and javelin throwing—so the multitude of different instrumental gestures are explored in the junior orchestra and in individual practicing. Songs with two parts in Group A and two parts in Group B in juxtaposition alternate with four-part catches by Mozart or Haydn—a lively exercising with variety and joy.

Sixth Grade

In sixth grade, at last music makes sense. The children are able to grasp more than they let on. They understand the cadence of chords in the same way as they practice the beauty of language. The sentient element is supplemented by the beginning thought capacity; Steiner points to the tendons, growing stronger, and the strength of bones that is felt. Orpheus enters the child: music itself! The child understands, through musical laws, that everything in the world is connected, and will explore these laws all around him. Geometry has prepared the interest in form. Now is the point in the Waldorf curriculum for the first scientific subject to be introduced: acoustics, leading to the anatomy of the larynx. Knowing the importance that the study of the larynx has in the process of the sixth grader's budding thinking activity brings the teacher to an understanding of the musical basis of scientific thought.

At the same time, the building of a simple eight-stringed lyre or a monochord is carried out. The entire nervous system has opened up to let the astral body stream in, ultimately forming "the lyre of Apollo" in the child going from sixth to eighth grade. A very sensitive description of this process is given by Steiner in *The Kingdom of Childhood*: "The astral body comes in along the nerve fibers from without inwards . . . it unites itself chemically with the organism, with all the tissues of the physical and etheric body."[3] In another connection, Steiner speaks of the coming in of the musical octave.

In order to understand the individual's connection to the very spirit of music, we should get to know biographical descriptions of great musicians. Also in sixth grade, the children's voices become one, for the first time. All children, boys and girls alike, speak with the same timing, most exactingly. This has to do with the stabilizing of the rhythm of breath and heartbeat, and the readiness of the organism to receive the soul body, as described above. The child only now begins to understand the laws of improvisation. Three-part madrigals and rounds in canon form are practiced, many in Latin, leading to the experience of the fugal canon when voices enter at different tonal levels. It has become a laudable custom in many Waldorf schools to involve sixth graders in the production of Gluck's opera *Orpheus*, or Mozart's *The Magic Flute*. The first tender musical steps now take a leap!

Seventh Grade

It is exciting to turn in seventh grade to musical ballads with two students singing the narrative and all joining in the chorus: *John Barleycorn*, sea chanteys, a selection of folk songs. Musical form is studied along with three- and four-part songs. Seventh graders should go to concerts often!

Eighth Grade

As to eighth grade, from now onwards it goes fast. The astral body takes hold in the student. Most children at this age now undergo the change of voice, becoming altos or tenors or basses. This enables a tentative road from polyphonic music to the four-part chorale. Do not force it if voices are not ready; give the boys individually a six-week break when they reach the change of voice.

The child realizes that everywhere one can find musical motifs. *The Master Singers of Nuremberg* by Richard Wagner is a great experience of the motif of each person, of each situation. "Am I, too, a motif? Do I not have my part to play?" Socially something happens—what hits the child is the feeling of taking something on. His own destiny is coming towards him with a question: Who are you, and how does your motif fit into the theme of others around you? In music, we realize, everything fits. With the voice having changed, or still changing, one thing becomes clear to each student: there is good purpose in limitation. "My contributing as an alto voice gives depth to the soprano part others sing." It is an inner realization that happens at different moments for different individuals. As four-part songs enter in, or Brucknerian extended chords, in which each voice part counts, that realization is a life-saver, because "now I know that I am needed." There can be no feelings of isolation, nor thoughts of taking one's own life, in a time of otherwise serious self-scrutiny.

The High School Years

This sense of belonging to a larger whole leads to the need for joining a high school or community choir, especially from grade nine onwards. The opportunity must also be given for an outlet for the sense of beat in bands or jazz groups, as the beat stirs from *within*. In some schools, ballroom dancing is introduced.

In tenth grade the orchestral experience is most in the foreground. The school orchestra is the main musical fulfillment and was especially suggested by Rudolf Steiner for the tenth grade. Then follows solo singing—a real test for eleventh graders—and the practice of distinguishing different musical styles, which can be developed to a faculty that discerns instantaneously on hearing a few bars of any type of music. In other words, the student is prepared for life and its choices, and for the beat of destiny, about which much more could be said!

Only having touched on the methods of a musical approach for the very young, and the kindergarten child, this talk mainly focuses on the lower school music curriculum. The brief hour allowed for indications only. It may, however, be of help to see these indications as a diagram. This diagram shows clearly that the musical experience of the child falls into three periods, notably different in kind: First—and this begins already in the kindergarten—it is the mood of the fifth that prevails. Then, for the middle school child, all is brought into the diatonic tonality in the major and minor harmony experiences. For the high schooler, the elements of beat and the chromatic twelve tones lead out into life.

We might draw a kind of overview/diagram in the following way:

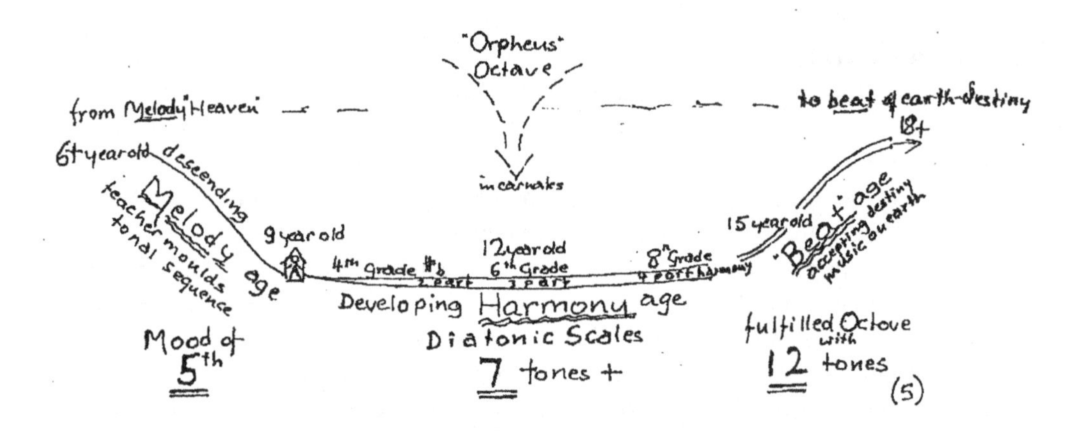

Notes

1. Rudolf Steiner, *Practical Advice to Teachers*, lectures given in Stuttgart, August 21–September 5, 1919 (London: Rudolf Steiner Press), p. 20.

2. Rudolf Steiner, *Waldorf Education for Adolescence: Supplementary Course—The Upper School*, Lecture IV (Forest Row, England: Steiner Schools Fellowship Publication, 1965), p. 50.

3. Rudolf Steiner, *The Kingdom of Childhood*, lectures given in Torquay, August, 12–20 1924 (London: Rudolf Steiner Press, 1974), Lecture 6, p. 108-109.

Christof-Andreas Lindenberg is a long-time co-worker in the Camphill Movement who has been a musician since his earliest years. As a curative music teacher he taught in the grades, chiefly at St. Johns School at Camphill Scotland and elsewhere, on and off in the last five decades, and has advised Waldorf and special teachers on methods of the applied music curriculum.

The Importance of the Mood of the Fifth in Modern Primary Education

JANA HAWLEY

The following article is excerpted from the first three chapters of Jana's paper submitted in May of 2009 in partial fulfillment of the requirements for her Master of Science in Education degree from Sunbridge College. Jana offers us a thorough explanation of the nature and qualities of mood of the fifth music and places it in the context of the evolution of human consciousness. She also presents a detailed explanation of music theory to aid in understanding the technical aspects of mood of the fifth music. While Jana's focus in the paper was on the primary grades, the excerpts offered here speak directly to the work of the early childhood educator.

Introduction

The successful unfolding of a conscious, free, and independent adult is the goal of Waldorf education, and this depends strongly on the child's developing a firm foundation in the early years of school. As Waldorf educators, our task is to aid in the creation of this firm foundation.

In my work as a Waldorf music teacher over the past two decades, I have found that children before the age of nine years need a unique kind of pedagogical practice. In the first and second grades the children are more open, more intuitive, and have fewer filters through which they view the world. Therefore, the teacher must take great responsibility for the material that is brought, for it nourishes the students' souls just as the food they bring in their lunch baskets nourishes their physical bodies. They drink in whatever is presented, and it becomes their own being. Just as healthy digestion takes place in a comfortable and nurturing atmosphere—like the family dining table—the children will more readily, easily, and thoroughly partake of, and digest, the material and activities of a lesson if there is a comfortable and nurturing mood set in the room and in the students at the beginning of the lesson. This mood, for the early primary years, may be called the mood of the fifth, and though this refers to a state of consciousness, it can best be described in musical terms.

Most Waldorf teachers have heard this term "mood of the fifth" in connection with the music lesson or the repertoire of songs for kindergarten and grades one and two. However, it is important to keep in mind that for the child of age nine or younger, this mood should permeate the entire day, not just the music lesson or morning circle time, because it creates the right atmosphere for learning anything.

My motivation for writing on this topic has sprung from my work in the classroom, where I experience again and again the benefits of bringing this mood, and also from my work as an educator of teachers. For the past decade I have taught a course on the mood of the fifth to early childhood educators. In every course I have met strong resistance to this concept of the mood of the fifth, and especially to the music that embodies this concept. I believe this response comes partly from the shift in consciousness that the mood of the fifth brings about, to a very different state than our normal, adult consciousness. This reaction has led me to research and learn all I can about the mood of the fifth so that I can teach about it in such a way that it opens doors rather than preaches a dogma. It is one of the greatest challenges we face as educators of young children: to be truly in two states of consciousness at once, namely, the pre-nine-year-old state (mood of the fifth) and the adult state (mood of the third). It is my hope that by the time the reader has come to the end of this article, these terms will be filled with meaning, and the wish to educate children in this way will be firmly rooted in the reader with a conviction based on knowledge.

The Evolution of Consciousness

We usually think of consciousness only as the state of wakeful thinking. In Lecture VI of *Study of Man*, Rudolf Steiner speaks of three states of consciousness in which we are immersed during our waking life: wakefulness, dreaminess, and sleepiness. He explains that we are awake in that we think and know, we are dreaming in that we feel, and we are sleeping in our doing. He states that these states of consciousness are evidence of the activity of the spiritual nature of the human being—that we find conditions of consciousness in the activity of the human spirit just as we find forces of sympathy and antipathy in the activity of the human soul. He says, "If we consider the human being from the spiritual point of view we must lay the chief stress on discovering the conditions of consciousness."[1]

Furthermore, Steiner asserts that human consciousness is in an ongoing process of evolution traceable through consecutive historical and cultural periods, and that it is especially visible through the study of the history of the arts and music. In fact, he goes as far as to say, "The facts of human evolution are expressed in musical development more clearly than anywhere else."[2] Therefore, it seems we can trace the development, or evolution, of consciousness and thus the development of the activity of the human spirit by studying the history of music, its forms, and its theories.

We now embark on a journey through the ages of humankind and its music, beginning with ancient India and continuing through ancient Persia, ancient Mesopotamia, ancient Greece and Rome, and ending with the modern age, the Anglo-Saxon/Germanic. These ages form an important theoretical construct in Steiner's view of the evolution of consciousness. He traces this evolution from the catastrophic destruction of the great Atlantean civilization, when the bearers of the ancient mystery wisdom migrated across Europe and Asia and settled in different areas. The most exalted leader settled with a small group of followers in central Asia, and from this colony, initiates were sent out to found the great civilizations listed above. Through his description of migration and colonization, Steiner connects the Atlantean consciousness with the present-day human consciousness in an unbroken stream, allowing for a consistent thread of development to be followed through the ancient ages and into modern history.

The Musical Moods from Ancient to Modern Cultures

Ancient India: the mood of the seventh. During the age of ancient India, the human being dwelt in moods of the interval of the seventh. The music of this time was arranged according to successive sevenths, with smaller intervals being as yet unknown. There are authentic remains of ancient musical traditions still surviving among indigenous cultures that give an indication of the transporting, ecstatic experience of this kind of music based on sevenths. One of these musical traditions, the gamelan orchestras of Indonesia, gives us a readily available way to experience this music for ourselves through recordings and increasingly-widespread live performances. The gamelan uses a scale based on sevenths, the slendro scale, which is created by stacking pure, or natural, sevenths one on top of another until the cycle completes itself by returning to the starting tone, and then by compressing all of these tones into one octave via octave transposition. The resulting scale has five equally spaced tones, with each interval being somewhat larger than our current major second and slightly smaller than our current minor third. This scale gives rise to music that is transporting even to our modern-day consciousness, especially when used in the traditional, cyclical compositional style of most gamelan repertoire. Because it has no ground tone and no tension between the pitches that would bring the urgency of needing resolution, this music has a floating, transcendent, and ecstatic quality.

The music of the ancient Indian age, with its sounding interval of the natural seventh, reflected the state of human consciousness at that time, a state typified (and also expressed) by the human relationship to both the material world and the spiritual worlds. Human beings at this time felt that the physical world was all illusion and deception. To find reality, which to them meant finding the imprint of the spiritual world, human beings had to turn to inner experience. For it was the inner presence of divinity, the primal source of being, that dispelled illusion, made things real. So although they felt themselves a part of the physical world, they believed it to be illusory, and there was a distinct turning away from it, along with a desire to be transported to the world of the spirit. Through hearing the music of the sevenths they felt themselves to be at once standing on the earth and at the same time experiencing the world of the spirit. A great spirit took hold of them and filled them inwardly the moment they participated in music. "When they [human beings of the ancient Indian age] made music they were transported completely beyond themselves; they were within the great, all-pervading spirituality of the universe in an absolute motion. They were being moved."[3] Saying "I experience music" at this time was the same as saying "I feel myself in the spiritual world," and the spiritual world at that time held more of a feeling of reality than did the physical world upon which they stood. Human beings of this age received religious instruction merely by being taught this music of the sevenths. All music based on sevenths was evidence of the existence of the spiritual world, though it was not proof of material existence, and did not support or enlighten the relationship of the human being to the physical world.

Ancient Persia: the mood of the sixth. During the age of ancient Persia, human beings were arriving at the idea that the external reality of the natural world was an image of the divine, and should be embraced and transformed by human endeavor rather than shunned as illusion. "The conviction gradually grew within him that there are two worlds: the world of the good Spirit in which a man can immerse himself, and the world which has to be worked upon,"[4] and they realized they could receive from the world of the spirit the ideas and concepts that they would need in order to transform the world. However, they failed to find concrete evidence of the spiritual at work in nature, and were aware only of nature's resistance to their own work, causing them to regard the two worlds as divided by an immeasurable abyss. The change in human awareness of the world from the illusory, dream-like perception of the ancient Indian consciousness to a world that is split into two irreconcilable polarities was expressed by the tone systems of the music of this period.

The scales used in ancient Persian music were based on the naturally-occurring sixth of the overtone series, a sixth that is very different in quality from either the major or minor sixth of our present-day tone system. As with the seventh in ancient India, a stack of sixths over several octaves was compressed into the space of one octave by octave transposition, giving rise to scales that demonstrated the duality of experience of the ancient Persian, in that the ascending scale and the descending scale were no longer identical. As Heiner Ruland describes in *Expanding Tonal Awareness,*

> *The scale becomes one-sided—it can only embody one path, one aspect. The tone system contains the entire world, but it cannot be grasped from one direction alone, or from a single aspect. The scale is subject to the laws of time, is changeable, it has a beginning and an end.*[5]

The ascending and descending scales took on different characteristics, with the ascending bringing a minor mood, as if the darkness from the depths of the uncontrollable natural world were welling up. In contrast, the descending brought more of a major mood, as if the light from the heights of the spiritual world were gently falling on humanity. These opposing movements "throw us into entirely different worlds. . . we lose the middle that binds the two spheres together, we lose our center within ourselves."[6]

Ancient Mesopotamia: the mood of the fifth. Finally, in ancient Mesopotamia, human beings were able to find the laws of the spirit expressed in nature. They observed the movement of the planets and saw rhythms and patterns in these movements. They observed the growth of plants, the migration of animals, and the rotation of the seasons, and for all of these natural processes and their relation to one another and to humanity, human beings gradually built up a science. This was not a rational, abstract science, but rather an "imaginative wisdom drawn from the world of the senses."[7] In Steiner's words, "It became clear to them that there was a great wisdom governing all natural processes; that everything happened in accordance with great laws."[8] The "trouble" was that now the only means they had of observing the world were their sense experiences. They had lost the natural clairvoyance of the earlier ages that had allowed the human being to penetrate beyond the sense world.

However, when humanity lost the ability to perceive clairvoyantly and became more reliant on the senses, an inner path to reconnecting with the divine was revealed. As in the previous two ages, the tone structures built on the seventh and the sixth had the capacity to transport human beings, inevitably leading them out of themselves to unite with the spirit, rather than awakening an inner experience of themselves in the world. In the Mesopotamian epoch, experiencing the inner self first became a possibility, and the interval of the pure fifth, especially the descending fifth, gave humanity its first opportunity to find itself in musical experience. The ascending fifth still carried them back outside of themselves. Ruland concisely describes the effects of these intervals:

> *Thus, the fifth is the only interval in which we can weave back and forth between experiencing ourselves from within and from without. We remain outside of ourselves in the sixth and the seventh. In the fourth, third and second we remain in ourselves. In the fifth there is a breathing between within and without . . . thus the fifth with its breathlike alternation . . . is the earliest interval of musical self-discovery.*[9]

The pure fifth upon which the music of this Mesopotamian age was based, with its simple ratio of 2:3, was the first interval used in this musical explanation of the evolution of consciousness that is still in use today. Unlike the seventh and the sixth of antiquity, our modern-day fifth bears the same graceful, geometric proportion as the one used by the ancient Egyptians. The tone system built then has also survived into the present. In fact, it still forms the basis of classical music theory. Just as the stack of sevenths led to a scale with five equally spaced tones, and the stack of sixths to a scale of ten tones with opposing properties in its ascending and descending manifestations, a stack of fifths over seven octaves led to a cycle of twelve tones, a twelve-fold division of the octave. Rudolf Steiner addressed this in *The Inner Nature of Music and the Experience of Tone*:

> *The great mystery of man was revealed in the circle of fifths—all spiritual experience resulted from the awareness that the number of planets was contained in seven scales, and the number of signs of the zodiac was contained in the twelve fifths within the seven scales.*[10]

This twelve-fold division is what we know of today as the chromatic division of the octave into twelve equally spaced tones.

Ancient Greece and Rome: the mood of the fourth. The ancient Greeks began to search more within themselves for the connection to the spiritual world that the Mesopotamians found in observing the workings of the spirit in nature. A shift was gradually made, away from looking for answers from the natural world and toward looking for answers from within. According to Steiner, the task of the ancient Greeks was to take unfinished nature and impress upon it their human vision and creativity through art. The ancient Greeks also drew ideas about human relationships and society from their own inner life experience and ideas rather than looking to the natural world, the stars, and the changing seasons for guidance.

As the musical intervals became smaller, they allowed human consciousness to become more self-aware and self-directed. The interval of the fourth brought human beings to the threshold of this experience. In Steiner's words, the fourth "arises at the dividing line between the experience of the fifth of the outer world and the experience of the third in man's inner being."[11]

Standing on this threshold of the self, human beings observed themselves still from outside in the realm of the spirit, but realized they could be human and participate in the spiritual world at one and the same time. "He stands precisely at the border of his humanness, retaining it, yet viewing it from the other side."[12]

Several different tone systems with their related scales were created during this age. The first and most important one for our purposes was similar in form and construct to the tone systems of the preceding ages in that it was built out of a stack of intervals—in this case the fourth—and the tones were then compressed into one octave. This system had many of the same characteristics as the Mesopotamian system because the interval of the fourth and the interval of the fifth created the same stack of tones, since an ascending fifth will arrive at the same pitch as a descending fourth and *vice versa*. So the string of tones was the same, although the quality of the two intervals themselves brought quite different moods. Ruland tied this mood to self-revelation:

> *If I invert a fifth to make a fourth, a revelation of the world—or of the spiritual in the world—becomes a revelation of my own inner nature. Here we arrive musically at that stage of development where, in the Greek world, the old, naively received mystery wisdom was transformed into philosophy and independent thought.*[13]

Another tone system developed during the Greek age used a radial principle for constructing the scale rather than the cyclic, or stacking, principle of the preceding ages. This radial principle arose out of the overtone series, in which a series of tones radiated out from one originating tone, unfolding in ever-smaller steps. In the fourth octave of the overtone series we find a string of seven tones already ordered in gradually decreasing seconds within the space of a single octave. This scale prepared the way for human beings to experience the smaller intervals of the third and the second, leading human consciousness further into the inner realms and the possibility of awakening to a true self-consciousness.

The cyclic system of fourths flourished and was carried over into the medieval church modes, while the radial system declined in use, not to return until the beginning of the next age when the experience of the third began to transform the music of Western Europe.

Anglo-Saxon and Germanic (Modern): the mood of the third. The people of this age, in which we are now living, have not only impressed their inner nature on matter as the ancient Greeks did, but they have also discovered the laws of nature and used them to alter the world. They have descended far into materialism and the physical plane, and have done everything possible to conquer it. Through this descent to the physical plane they have gradually lost their connection with the spiritual world. According to Steiner, only the physical world exists now for most people, and from now on humankind will only gradually become more spiritual again.

The interval of the third brings the personal, inner side of human experience to expression for the first time. Through consciousness of the third, music ceased to be a more-than-human, spiritual concern and became a purely human concern—our music today reflects our daily existence. A completely subjective musical expression of mood is now possible.

The interval of the third stacked on itself does not reach beyond the space of one octave, so building a tone system in the cyclic manner of the ancient tone systems is not possible. The consciousness of the third leads instead to the musical triad that itself embodies a return to the radial scale of ancient Greece, a triad being a stack of two thirds of differing sizes. With the tonal system developed from the interval of the third, humanity uses the physical laws of the naturally occurring overtone series, raising the earthly to spiritual heights through the art of music. This tonal system presents a picture of how man can act now as a self-sufficient being with his own center, capable of radiating out into the spiritual world.

> *The human being experiences the seventh, sixth, and fifth in a transported condition, he stands at the boundaries of his own being in the fourth, he dwells within himself in the third. When man's inner life intensifies he will experience the second and finally he will become sensitive to the single tone—these are matters that lie in the future.*[14]

Evolutionary Phases Reflected in Child Development

The human being recapitulates the evolution of consciousness in his own biographical development. In ancient India (mood of the seventh), there existed a state of consciousness that did not differentiate between the human being and the spiritual world. When the human being sang, he was one with the spiritual world, in the same way that an infant does not and cannot differentiate at all between himself and his mother or the world.

During the ancient Persian age (mood of the sixth), the human being explored the physical world and began to transform it through his own effort, finding a relationship to the earth and transforming himself in the process, just like a toddler beginning to explore the physical world and in so doing finding a relationship to it, discovering what it is to be incarnated in a physical body.

In the Ancient Mesopotamian age (mood of the fifth) human beings "feel at home in an earthly frame for the first time, although with wide open spaces; we breathe the air and stand on firm ground."[15] The human being felt at home on the earth while still able to be transported to the spiritual world. We see a similar gesture in young children as they find a relationship between the physical and the spiritual worlds, leaving the spiritual world and beginning to feel at home in their physical body, although their true home is still in the spiritual world. By bringing the mood of the fifth to young children, we as teachers help them bring their spiritual home into their physical home, and more importantly help them to breathe between the two. This creates a pathway between the physical and spiritual worlds that will serve as a doorway for their entire lives.

Steiner stresses the importance of the breath in relationship to the interval of the fifth. According to him, in the experience of the fifth, the human being

> *still felt united with what lived in his breath. He said to himself . . . "I breathe in, I breathe out . . . The musical element, however, does not live in me at all; it lives in inhalation and exhalation." Man felt always as if he were leaving and returning to himself in the musical experience.*[16]

In the modern child the process of incarnation, or physical penetration, is accelerated and intensified, and the breathing back into the spiritual world is inhibited by a multitude of environmental factors. These factors include sensory overload, dietary sensitivities, pollution of all kinds, lack of rhythm, and sleep interference. Imbalances of in-breath or out-breath result in children who are driven too deeply into their bodies too soon and who never feel at home in their physical bodies. These imbalances can be seen in physical illnesses such as asthma, allergies, insomnia, hyperactivity, anxiety, and depression. It is one of our primary tasks as educators to cultivate healthy breathing both in the physical body and in the soul life of the child.

Music Theory

There are several music theory concepts that will help the non-musically-literate reader to grasp the actual music of the mood of the fifth. Learning some basic music vocabulary such as scale, interval, overtone, and pentatonic, and discovering how to experience some of these sounds in a practical way, will aid readers in their understanding of this article, as well as give them tools to create mood of the fifth music of their own, should they wish to.

Intervals. The spaces between different musical tones are called intervals. In the C major scale of contemporary western music there are tones that are named with letters: c′, d′, e′, f′, g′, a′, b′, and c″ (the low c and the second-octave high c are differentiated by the use of ′or ″). The tones can also be named using solfege syllables: *Do, re, mi, fa, sol, la, ti*, and *Do*. Between each pitch going stepwise up or down the scale there is the interval of either a large or small second. If one begins with c′, or *Do*, and rises up to each consecutively higher tone, the intervals get larger and farther apart, and are named the third, fourth, fifth, sixth, seventh, and octave. This is illustrated in the following figure:

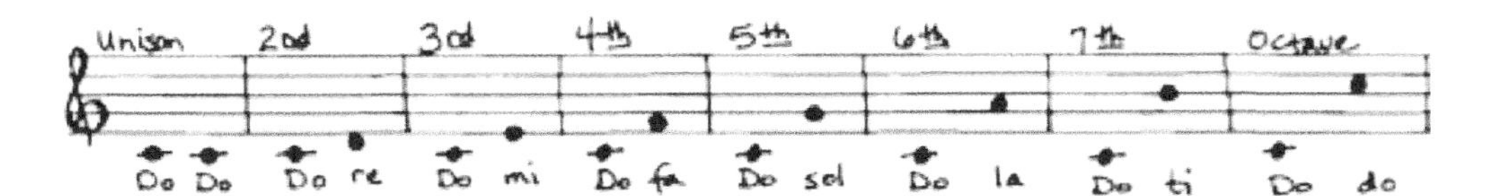

Thus, moving from *Do* to *re* creates the interval of a second, from *Do* to *mi* a third, from *Do* to *fa* a fourth, and so on. The intervals all have their particular character or mood, discernible when heard in a line of melody as consecutively sounding tones and also when played simultaneously, creating a harmonically sounding interval. As an exercise to develop the ear for the musical intervals, and the sensitivity to the different qualities inherent in each interval, we can sing the series *Do-re, Do-mi, Do-fa, Do-sol, Do-la, Do-ti, Do-do*, slowly, holding each new tone longer than the repeated *Do*. Taking the exercise further, we can have a control group or individual hold the low *Do* as a drone tone while another group or individual slowly sings the complete ascending scale, holding each new tone and letting it settle into place with the drone tone before moving on to the next tone. Especially in this last exercise, we get a feeling for the distinct qualities of each harmonically sounding interval, their relative consonance or dissonance to the ear, and which are more comfortable to sing and to hear. We also notice which intervals cause discomfort and are almost impossible to keep in tune for any length of time, as the pull towards resolving to a more consonant interval is so strong. To hear and develop an inner experience of the true intervals, it is important to sing them or to use an unfretted string instrument to play them.

The Overtone Series. The interval of the fifth is pleasing, as it sounds more consonant than any other interval except the unison or the octave. The reason for this can best be shown by referring to the ancient Greek discovery of the overtone or harmonic series. The harmonic series was discovered by Pythagoras in the sixth century BC as he was observing how the hanging weights in a blacksmith shop produced different pitches depending on the length of rope from which they were suspended. If the rope lengths were in simple proportions to each other, the tones produced were more consonant. This observation led Pythagoras to conduct experiments on the monochord, a single-stringed instrument. By dividing the string at different points along its length, he found how string length proportions give rise to different pitches creating a series of intervals, with the fundamental tone produced by sounding the whole length of the string. These experiments led Pythagoras to uncover the series illustrated below, which holds true for any length of string.

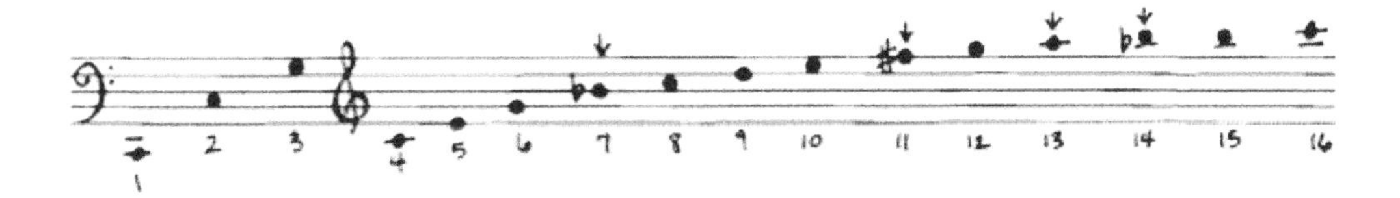

This was the first scientifically provable, mathematically-derived natural law that Pythagoras found in his quest for cosmic order expressed in the natural world. The interval of the fifth is produced by stopping the string at one third of its length and sounding the shorter length, then stopping the string at the halfway point and sounding that. So the proportion of half the string to one-third the string produces the interval of the fifth, while playing the full string in comparison to half the string produces the interval of the octave. As the string is divided into smaller consecutive sections of one quarter, one fifth, and so on, new pitches are produced which create new intervals from the pitch of the full string. We find that the simpler the proportion, the more consonant the interval. And the intervals can be named after their proportions, so an octave is named 1:2, a fifth is named 2:3, a fourth is named 3:4 and so on. The fifth has the simplest proportions of any interval except the octave. Thus it is the most consonant of intervals, with a pure, almost crystalline tone quality. However, it has an almost empty, cold clarity and does not inspire either sympathy or antipathy in the listener. We, as adults living in the 21st century, want to fill it with something, with warmth and emotion. In particular, we want to add the third that will create a triad:

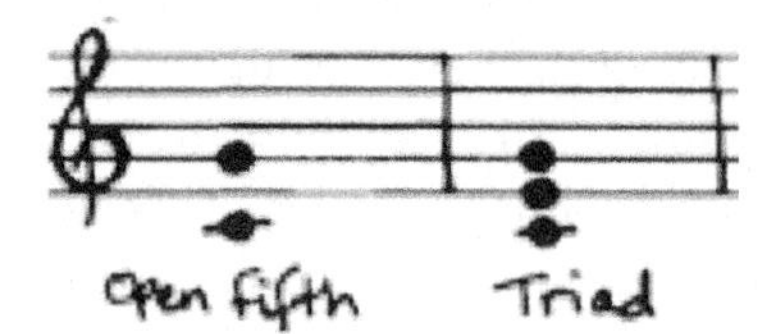

This is the common chord, so familiar to our ears, that carries feelings of happiness or sadness, but definitely evokes an emotional response. The fifth is more remote, giving form and structure to music. Thus compositions that are created using the fifth as their guiding principle and main building block give rise to music that does not engage the emotions but brings form and clarity, allowing the breath to move freely through the form without getting caught by a feeling.

The Mood of the Fifth Pentatonic Scale. The term *pentatonic* means five tones (*penta:* five; *tonic:* tone), or a scale with five tones that fit within the range of one octave. There are many different kinds of pentatonic scales that have been used world-wide throughout history. (For a wonderful experience of the pentatonic scale, go to YouTube and type in "bobby mcferrin pentatonic scale.") The tones used in mood of the fifth are found in the pentatonic scale created by stacking fifths on top of each other, starting with the lowest tone of the average human voice and rising to the highest average singable tone, which gives the five tones G d'a'e'' and b''. This series of tones is illustrated below.

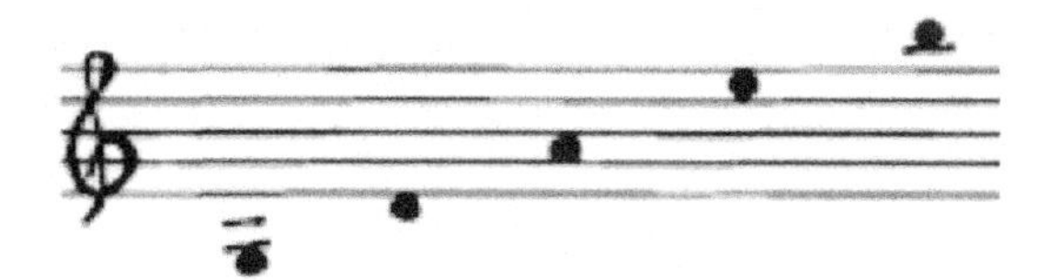

This is the compass of the average human voice, written in the female range—for men it would all sound one octave lower. The tones are then transposed to fit within the space of one octave. Thus, b″is moved down one octave to b′while G moves up to g′and we add the octaves of d′ and e″, arriving at the seven tones of a pentatonic scale. This scale is still considered pentatonic even though there are seven tones, because only five tones are present within any one octave (see Figure 5).

Steiner suggests that the real music of the mood of the fifth would have used these tones only, sung with the wide spacing between all the tones, with the smallest interval used being the fifth. If we experiment with this concept with a group of singers, we find that it definitely changes the state of consciousness from one of wakefulness and interest to one more akin to being on the edge of sleep, or of being lifted away from a foundation of self-awareness and swimming through the airy reaches with no place to land, no sense of the ground, and no way to be able to say, "This is me and I am singing." It is more a feeling of *being sung*, which is exactly how Steiner describes the fifth consciousness:

> *In the music of the fifths, a human being felt lifted out of himself. . . . when he experienced fifths, he would have been inclined to say, "The angel in my being is beginning to play music. The muse in me speaks." "I sing" was not the appropriate expression. It became possible to say this only when the experience of the third emerged, making the whole musical feeling an inward experience; the human being then felt that he himself was singing.*[17]

The kind of discomfort experienced by creating music that can transport us to this older state of consciousness can be acute for some, and can explain the resistance some people have toward the music of the mood of the fifth. And yet, this is the state in which children under the age of nine are living all the time. It is our task to understand it, and to be there with them so we can journey together toward the modern-day consciousness. Perhaps our most difficult task is to have one foot in each world, to keep our adult state of consciousness intact and still be creating the appropriate mood for the children in our classroom.

Composing in the Mood of the Fifth. There are specific compositional techniques for creating music that will bring the mood of the fifth to the classroom. The most important concept is that the whole arrangement of tones turns around the axis of the center tone, the a′, so that the boundaries of low and high are each a fifth away from the center tone, and the melodic movement is from center to periphery and back again, rather than rising from a ground tone and returning with a feeling of finality. Mood-of-the-fifth songs do not give that feeling of arriving home to a settled place by the end. They keep a sense of suspension, of not ending, of merely an in-breath turning into an out-breath and back again. True mood of the fifth melodies embody this breathing process. Another kind of breathing may happen within the text, if a song alternates between the syllabic style, in which each syllable of a word is sung on its own tone, and the melismatic style, in which many tones are sung on one syllable, or hummed. The alternation of the syllabic style with the melismatic style also lets us breathe between a more awake, wordy state and a more dreamy, flowing state.

This breathing between polarities of high and low, and of syllabic and melismatic, is a key to composing in the mood of the fifth. Other polarities to consider are soft and loud, fast and slow, ascending and descending melodic movement, and beat-oriented rhythm contrasted with more chant-like rhythm, such as when the rhythm is taken from the words themselves. A melody may have the feeling of duple meter, or two divisions of a beat, such as in a march, or triple meter, or three divisions of a beat, such as in a waltz. Some songs have alternating meters to keep the sense of the breath alive, breathing between the feeling of duple and triple meter, not becoming fixed in one division of time that can make a repetitive beat start to drive the music. In fact, mood-of-the-fifth music should not have too strong a sense of beat. If a song with a strong beat is used, it is healthy to follow it with a piece that is less rhythmic or metered, in order to maintain the breathing mood of the fifth.

This link of breathing to music based in fifths is of paramount importance to our understanding of why this kind of music is so important for young children, especially in the light of Steiner's first pedagogical lecture in *Study of Man.* Here he emphasizes that one of the teacher's most urgent tasks is to help the students learn to breathe: "Amongst all the relationships which man has to the external world, the most important of all is breathing."[18] Again, "The breathing is the most important mediator between the outer physical world and the human being who is entering it;"[19] and also ". . . [T]he child cannot yet breathe in the right inner way, and education will have to consist in teaching the child to breathe rightly."[20] We find in the mood of the fifth an aid to this task of educating the breath, not just the physical breathing of air into our lungs, but the breathing of all of our senses, of our consciousness, of our soul forces of sympathy and antipathy.

Conclusion

It is my hope that this detailed treatment, with both spiritual and musical motivations explained, will have clearly illustrated why an understanding of the mood of the fifth is so important for educators of the young child, and that it will also motivate and assist teachers to work with the mood of the fifth.

Notes

1. Rudolf Steiner, *Study of Man* (London: Rudolf Steiner Press, 1966), Lecture VII, p. 98. This lecture series is also available from SteinerBooks as *The Foundations of Human Experience.*

2. Rudolf Steiner, *The Inner Nature of Music and the Experience of Tone* (Anthroposophic Press, 1983), Lecture VI, p. 70.

3. Ibid., p. 70.

4. Rudolf Steiner, "The Post-Atlantean Culture-Epochs," Sept. 1, 1906, in *At the Gates of Spiritual Science* (London: Rudolf Steiner Press 1986) Lecture 11, p. 100.

5.Heiner Ruland, *Expanding Tonal Awareness* (London: Rudolf Steiner Press, 1992), p. 72.

6. Ibid., p. 75.

7. Ibid. p. 76.

8. Steiner, "The Post-Atlantean Culture-Epochs," p. 101.

9. Ruland, op. cit., p. 75.

10. Steiner, *The Inner Nature of Music and the Experience of Tone,* p. 69.

11 Ibid., p. 61.

12. Ibid., p. 62.

13. Ruland, op. cit., p. 57.

14. Steiner, *The Inner Nature of Music and the Experience of Tone,* p. 71.

15. Ruland, op. cit., p. 57.

16. Steiner, *The Inner Nature of Music and the Experience of Tone,* p. 55.

17. Ibid., p. 51-52.

18. Rudolf Steiner, *Study of Man*, Lecture 1, p. 20.

19. Ibid., p. 20.

20 Ibid., p. 21.

Jana Hawley taught music, served as class teacher in the middle school, and regularly taught morning lesson blocks at the Whidbey Island Waldorf School from 1992-2006. Since moving to Green Meadow Waldorf School, she has taught lower school music for Grades 1-8, and became a class teacher in 2011. She also teaches at many Waldorf teacher training programs, including Sunbridge Institute, where she currently serves as Program Director of Waldorf Elementary Teacher Education.

PART THREE

The World of Tone: Singing, Sounding, Listening

The Influence of Music on the Young Child

CAROL KELLY

In this article, which originally appeared in Renewal, *Carol Kelly suggests to parents and teachers ways of supporting the young child's healthy incarnation through music that respects and preserves the child's delicate sensory organism and sense of wonder.*

A unique and enlightening idea in Waldorf education is that child development is a reflection of the stages of human evolution and that a curriculum can be created that meets the needs of the child at each age. The first grader, then, who is full of imagination and not yet very aware of time and space, is given fairy tales coming out of the dream consciousness of early humanity. And the seventh grader, inquisitive and ready to step into the world, learns about the explorers, the discoverers, and the great artists of the Renaissance. Those of us who teach in Waldorf schools see the nourishing pedagogical effects that come about when the child meets the right subject at the right time.

In the child's experience of music, this same principle pertains. It is important that we, as parents and teachers, approach music with the same pedagogical insight that we apply to other influences. The infant and the growing child should be exposed to music for which they are ready, music which comes from the period of human history corresponding to their own stages of development. With great care and attentiveness, we must protect the open musical "innocence" of the young child. A protective nurturing is needed to keep the innate musicality of the child intact long enough for it to develop to the highest degree possible.

This is especially critical and difficult today. The sound-space around us and our children is constantly invaded by noise, mechanical sounds, imitations of music, and by electronic reproductions that bring the whole gamut of musical idioms, often unbidden, into our personal environment.

If we observe a baby, we see at once that she is all head and "tummy." The infant is a picture of roundness, a reflection of the earth, at one with its environment. Already in the mother's womb, the fetus is in a state of "super-hearing," in tune with the mother's voice and with her heartbeat. The baby, then, comes with a highly-developed sense of hearing. She takes in all the sounds around her with no protection and with no possibility of shutting out the undesirable ones. Rudolf Steiner says that a little child is entirely a sense organ and absorbs and is molded by the sights and sounds which come into her sphere. This absorption is not a conscious activity, but has a powerful effect on the child. Everything we say and do in the presence of such an open being has a significant impact.

Instinctively, mothers have been singing lullabies to their babies since the beginning of time, and this is the best, first musical "training." The more purely and simply the mother can sing, the better. Practicing on the sound "ng," like the end of the word "ring," is a good way to find the ideal tone. Mothers can hum or sing softly and in a flowing manner without specific melodies or rhythms. The infant, having just arrived from Heaven, is not ready for earthly melodies or music from mechanical music boxes. He needs to be let down gently to earth as if on a cloud. This helps the forming of the child's entire organism.

As Willi Aeppli writes in *The Development of the Human Senses:* "The small child hears music, for instance, less with the ear than with his whole body, which vibrates and lives in the musical element. His whole physical being is either in harmony or disharmony."[1]

The music that the older infant and the toddler hear should be beautiful in tone, flowing in movement, and uncomplicated in melody. The intervals (the spaces between the notes) should be large and open, fifths and sixths rather than semitones and seconds. The reason is that these larger intervals characterized music in the early stages of human evolution, and the young child, in terms of soul development, is in that same early epoch.

The best instruments to play for little children are the lyre, the harp, the pentatonic *klangspiel* (a little xylophone manufactured in Sweden by Choroi), and bells. These instruments do not demand technical musical training and allow any parent to play music for his or her child. A streaming or flowing rhythm is much better for the child than a set rhythm or pulse. This can come later. Listening to Javanese gamelan music or to the traditional music of India is a good way for parents to enter the open, cosmic musical space of the small child. Instruments of poor quality, as well as all recorded music, should be avoided.

Parents and teachers of children between the ages of three and five can often hear "cosmic" music naturally flowing from the children themselves as they are enchanted in quiet play. Many times I have tip-toed past my daughter's bedroom so as not to disturb the sweet song she was singing. I could hear a flowing, continuous melody based on a repeated phrase, with a rhythm that arose from her own breathing and from the words she sang. Such a moment is a golden opportunity for us to learn about music directly from our children.

These days, however, the enchantment is being broken all too soon, and it is more and more difficult for children to enter into the "stream of music." I was teaching music in the first grade recently when I experienced this most clearly. For this age group, pentatonic music, music based on a five-note scale, is most appropriate. Thus, we were singing a lovely pentatonic song, "Look at the Snow Falling Down," and we were floating a piece of white silk in the air as "snow." Most of the children were singing purely and were really experiencing the falling of the imaginary snow. Then one little boy brought in his own imagination, which happened to be that of a machine gun. He began to "blast" everyone in the room, adding his own sound effects as he did so. The mood which had been carefully established was broken. More and more often, the wooden flutes the children learn to play become "guns."

At such moments, I think of the shepherd boy on the hill and of the music which poured forth so naturally out of his inner being and from his communion with nature. Once the sense of wonder and the ability enter into the "stream of music" have been lost, they are all but impossible to recapture. That is why, in Waldorf education, we go back to the beginning and try to preserve and protect these gifts from the earliest age onward.

If we look back to ancient times, we find many references to a pure, cosmic music descending from the heavens to the earth. The Greeks called it the *Musica Mundana* or the Music of the Spheres. According to Rudolf Steiner, music in early times was experienced as the activity of spiritual beings. Also, human beings' perception of music was much different than it is today. People were able to hear only large intervals such as the seventh (in Atlantean times) and the fourth and fifth (during Greek, Roman, and even early medieval times). While today we hear the interval of the third as harmonious, eight hundred years ago it was experienced as a discord.[2]

In modern music, we have "descended" into the smallest intervals possible, semitones and even electronically-produced microtones. We can wonder about our present soul condition and where this development of music will lead us.

For the young child, still at one with his environment and lacking self-consciousness, music should be played or sung with an awareness of its spiritual origins. The tones themselves exist outside of space and time and are brought to us through the medium of air. Then through a movement—a striking, blowing, or bowing—a sound is born and then received by human ears.

Adults can also "hear" music that is not sounding in the physical world. Composers do this much of the time. This music which adults hear inwardly has been shaped by the music they have heard in live performances and on recordings and by their education and cultural background. But in the young child, the inner musical space is still wide open and pure. We need to protect it well, lest it be violated and destroyed.

Teachers with long experience recognize that children today are less able to listen, to maintain attention, and to sing than they were, even ten or twenty years ago. This is no wonder, when we consider the bombardment of loud noises and unmusical sounds to which children and adults are subjected each day. Our ears do not have protective lids as our eyes do. We cannot close our ears, and so we endure innumerable harsh sounds constantly—traffic noise, electronic sounds, background music in public places, and so forth. We have little defense against this attack on our humanity, and we have actually adapted to it and accept it as normal. But we have paid the price. We have lost our ability to truly hear and to discern the false from the true, real music from "canned," live from "Memorex."

Heiner Ruland writes in his book *Expanding Tonal Awareness*: "What is really musical can only reveal itself when tone and interval are taken up into an inner experience, a conscious soul experience. For this to become possible, adults must retrain their ears, but we can help to preserve the listening capacities of children by our attentive tending of the sound environment from birth to school readiness."[3]

It is possible even today for us to protect our infants and young children from the barrage of noise and *ersatz* music which permeates our environment and to surround them with simple, beautiful, natural music. If we do this, the children will grow into their own musicality, playing and singing in joyful self-expression. And, as they grow older, they will be able to take up the creation and performance of music in a truly healing and creative way. Through our joyful making of music together with others, music can become once again the golden thread that weaves communities together, enhances our lives, and enriches our souls.

Notes

1. Willi Aeppli, *The Development of the Human Senses* (Forest Row, England: Rudolf Steiner Schools Fellowship).
2. Rudolf Steiner, *The Inner Nature of Music and the Experience of Tone* (Spring Valley, NY: Anthroposophic Press, 1983).
3. Heiner Ruland, *Expanding Tonal Awareness* (London: Rudolf Steiner Press, 1992).

Carol Kelly was a class teacher and music teacher in the Great Barrington and Hawthorne Valley Waldorf schools until 1998, when she entered the Seminary of The Christian Community. She was ordained in 2001 and currently works as a priest in Washington, DC. She leads a church choir, runs singing workshops, and directs The Christian Community children's camp where over one hundred children and young people come together for great singing and fun every August.

The Erosion of Listening

A Contemporary Crisis of Childhood

SHEILA PHELPS JOHNS

Sheila Johns shares some observations of how the sense of hearing may suffer in our modern world, and describes her work with grade-school children in helping to protect and heal this sense. The exercises she describes are not meant for use in the early childhood setting, but her article is an important reminder of the importance of nurturing the sense of hearing, as well as the ability to listen, and the necessity of protecting the infant's and young child's delicate sensory organism. This article is published with kind permission from the Association for Healing Education, healingeducation.org.

"Can you tell me again what we are supposed to do, Mrs. Johns?" I looked at the pale second grader with a mixture of exasperation and curiosity. How could she possibly have failed to hear the simple instructions I had just given to the class? She was actually looking directly at me the whole time I was speaking, which had been for less than thirty seconds. Withholding judgment, I leaned over to her and asked gently if she hadn't heard what I had just said. Now it was her turn to be exasperated. "Yes, Mrs. Johns, of course I *heard* what you said, I just wasn't *listening* to it!"

Our sense of hearing is one that is fairly well understood. Along with what our eyes perceive through our sense of sight, what our ears hear through our sense of hearing allows us to orient ourselves in space. Ambient sound helps us to make sense of our environment. We do hearing tests to make sure that children's auditory perceptions are in order, and we caution our young people against excessive use of earphones with the volume turned up because of concern about damage to their organs of hearing. Like sight, our ability to hear is based on the proper function of a physical mechanism, and when any aspect of that mechanism is faulty, our physical ability to hear is compromised.

Only there was nothing at all wrong with this second grader's sense of hearing. She confirmed that she had heard all that I said, so why had she not understood it?

In the more than ten years that have passed since that instructive conversation, I have seen demonstrated again and again the profound difference between our *physical* sense of hearing and our *soul* sense of listening.

What does it mean to listen to something? We speak of the "phenomenon of hearing," but we speak of the "activity of listening." Our sense of hearing gives us the physical possibility to take what we have heard *outwardly* and do something with it *inwardly*. Whether it is conscious or not, listening actually requires a decision to act. Within the aural realm, when we meet something that comes to us from *without*, with intentional activity from *within*, the result is listening. It is a meeting that takes place in our inner being, the result of soul activity that goes beyond our sense perception of hearing. And it is only through such an inner meeting that *understanding* can actually take place. The implications of this are profound, pointing as they do to listening as a soul capacity—a capacity that actually has nothing to do with our ears! Seen in this way, it is possible to gain new therapeutic insight into a fundamental human capacity that seems to be diminishing in our population at large at an alarming rate.

The full range of causes and consequences of the apparent decline in modern human beings' capacity to listen are too vast to be considered in this brief article, but it is possible to point to a few overarching themes and some possible ways of offering supportive remediation.

First, how can we more deeply understand the relationship of hearing to listening? It certainly could be said that any imbalance in the sense of hearing creates a potential compromise in the capacity to listen. But does this imply that better hearing means better listening? A growing number of children coming to us today suffer from hyper-acuity in their sense of hearing, which actually challenges their ability to listen. Why is that?

An infant, whose physical senses are wide open to the surrounding environment, has a need to monitor the multitude of sense impressions coming towards it. In the visual realm, the infant does this by closing its eyes. The amount of time an infant spends with its eyes closed is, in part, indicative of what percentage of visual impressions are indigestible to the infant. The closing of the eyes is a protective measure that is self-regulating. Regrettably, the human being does not possess a similar protective mechanism for the sense of hearing. The infant, who Rudolf Steiner described as "one large sense organ" is left entirely at the mercy of its surrounding in the realm of sound, and infants who are exposed to the average quantity and quality of sounds in our modern environment with no built-in mechanism to protect themselves may suffer effects on much deeper levels. Such experiences may, in fact, trigger a certain kind of inner shutting down, as the sound penetrates beyond the physical ears right into the core of its being.

Later on, we meet children who do not know how to properly "digest" the sounding world around them. This can lead to aural hyper-acuity in some children who have not learned to modulate the sounding world and who experience the plethora of sounds around them as an assault. In other children, it can lead to a listening faculty that has been largely shut down because of the repeated need for self-protection.

It is critical to educate parents about the importance of protecting the ears of the infant or young child from loud, excessive, or mechanical noise.

As with so many other developing faculties in young children, imbalances in the listening capacity require thoughtful therapeutic support from pedagogues and therapists as well. First and foremost, it is our task to provide opportunities for children to exercise their listening capacity for its own sake, rather than as only a means to an end. To start with, something as simple as creating a moment of silence in a room is a tremendous gift to modern children! This can be done at the beginning of any class or therapy session. I always invite a child or a class to close their eyes in order to enhance their sense of hearing in that blessed silence. This is a tall order for many of our children who have become so overly dependent on their visual sense that they find it nearly impossible to keep their eyes closed. Multiple repetitions of this basic activity may be required before children can allow themselves to live into this often-foreign aural landscape. Eventually, at the end of twenty or thirty seconds of such an exercise, the out-breathing in the room becomes almost palpable. Over time, children begin to crave these moments, and have often reminded me, if I forget to allow space for this activity. I remember a sixth grader who commented to me that his favorite part of orchestra class was the moment of silence right before the playing began, reflecting that it always gave him "goose bumps." Such experiences can indeed become "holy moments" for children.

Once children have learned how to be comfortable with silence, it is possible to take another step by asking them to "reach out" beyond the silence with their listening, to discover what they can hear. This is not an easy exercise for some children. We must recognize that the active gesture of listening is actually an opening out to the world. It is a gesture of expansion, which is actually the polar opposite gesture to the "shutting down" that for too many children has become a habitual reflex of self-protection against the excessive noise in our environment. It is important to have created a space where the children can feel safe to activate this inner faculty. Many children have never consciously engaged this capacity, and when they have the courage to do so, one can almost imagine a tender blossom unfolding toward the sun. Once engaged, it is remarkable how far a child's listening can actually extend.

A third exercise could be described as "willing the listening to move in the space toward a certain sound." Here we can observe another important distinction of listening. Our sense of hearing is indiscriminate. We hear whatever is sounding in our immediate environment. The activity of listening, on the other hand, requires discrimination. Discrimination in listening gives meaning to what is heard, which leads to the possibility for understanding. I may have the class sit quietly with eyes closed and simply get used to hearing me speak without being able to see me. (A few children are always amazed that they can still hear me, even though their eyes are closed!) Then I silently move to another area of the room. Out of the silence, I ask if they can still hear me and have them point to where in the room my voice is coming from. After a few more moves, I end up squarely behind them. I have now moved out of their visual space in front and have entered their actual listening space. From here, I challenge them to remain facing forward with their eyes closed and reach behind them with their listening. I then tell a little story—speaking, singing, or playing into that "back space" which has finally been activated.[1]

This exercise can be expanded to involve children moving unseen to various parts of the room. Whichever child I point to takes a turn making a small sound with an object or instrument, and the seated children must point in the direction of the sound or figure out who the "sound maker" was. A more sophisticated exercise involves making several distinct repeated sounds with simple instruments and having children focus their listening on only one pre-determined sound. This requires a more advanced type of discrimination where the child must begin to separate essential from inessential. This listening skill is at the heart of a child's ability to succeed in classroom-based education.

Such an introductory article would not be complete without the mention of one of the most valuable listening tools that can be used with children or adults, and that is the tone of the lyre. In my experience, the sounding of even a single lyre tone into a space awakens an immediate listening response. It would be the subject of another article to explore the possibility of nourishing the sense of hearing and the capacity to listen through the pedagogical and therapeutic use of the lyre and other "new" instruments, which have been specifically designed to free the musical tone where it can be met through our listening into the surrounding space.

A few years ago, I had an experience that gave me a profound appreciation of the listening challenges our children face in today's world. A concerned fourth grade teacher spoke to me about a boy who seemed unable to sing with the rest of the class. She hastened to explain that he had lost his mother to cancer just the previous summer. In working with him, I was not surprised to find that his very low choice of pitch was deliberate—it was simply too painful for him to sing in the higher register where he used to sing with his mother. Moved with compassion, I sensed that he was clearly an inwardly sensitive child by nature, and he responded immediately when I asked him to listen within, and then to sing whatever tone he heard inside, which I then matched with my voice and lyre. He loved this exercise of my confirmation of the tone that he had sounded, and over time I was able to coax the register up in increments until, gradually, feeling more confidence in himself, he was able to expand the range in which he was comfortable singing. It was truly a healing work for this child.

One day, after several months of this, he gave me a remarkable insight: I had asked him, as usual, to quiet himself and to listen within, and then to hum whatever tone was sounding in him. He listened for longer than usual and then, furrowing his brow, informed me that he was having a hard time hearing his tone that day. Determined, he listened again. Suddenly, out of the silence, he opened his eyes wide and exclaimed, "I know what the problem is! I've been playing a lot with my new Nintendo, and every time I listen today, I'm hearing the sound of that Nintendo, which is covering up the sound of my own tone!"

To what extent the "sounding brass and clanging cymbals" of our contemporary acoustic environment threaten to separate our children from the sounding of their own tone or their own voice or their own thoughts and feelings, we can hardly guess.

Ultimately, the deed of active listening has the power to open that realm to them again, to confirm their connection to their intrinsic selves and ultimately to allow them to embrace the world around them from within.

Note

1. In a series of lectures entitled *The World as Product of the Working of Balance* given in Dornach, Switzerland in November of 1914, Rudolf Steiner describes the three planes of the physical human body in space. In addition to the right/left dimension and the up/down dimension, we live in the world in the front/back dimension. Our eyes, located at the forefront of our faces, orient the visual space in front of us and give us knowledge about the world through what we can see. Our ears, on the other hand, located at the sides of our head, have the possibility to take in something of what lives in the unknown, unseen space behind us. The unconscious gesture of leaning back and cupping the ear in order to hear something reflects the relationship of this so-called "back space" to our capacity to listen.

Sheila Phelps Johns has worked with the lyre in the early grades for thirteen years at the Washington Waldorf School, where she is also a member of the Care Group. She has completed anthroposophic trainings in both instrumental and singing therapy. She works with music therapeutically at the school and through her private practice in Silver Spring, MD.

Reflections on the Importance of Singing

KAREN LONSKY

In this article, which appeared in Gateways *in an earlier version, Karen offers thoughts on the role of singing not only in the early childhood classroom but in our lives as developing human beings.*

Oh Music,
In your depths we deposit
Our hearts and souls;
You have taught us to see with our ears
And to hear with our hearts.
—Kahlil Gibran

I came across this verse in my notebook the other day while thinking about the importance of singing with children. It spoke to me immediately and I remembered moments in my life as evidence of the poet's words. "In your depths we deposit our hearts and souls. . ." Music is not only *taken* in by human beings; there is a response to what is heard, an inner resonance. Music can provide a pleasant experience, an uplifting experience, an emotional experience, or sometimes even an unpleasant experience. "You have taught us to see with our ears. . ." Who has not had the experience of a piece of music bringing to our mind's eye a fully-formed picture of a place or an event? ". . . And to hear with our hearts." This brings to me the memory of hearing Barber's "Adagio for Strings" for the first time and feeling my heart expand and lighten to the point where my senses seemed to draw me heavenward. What a powerful messenger music can be! It may create a bridge between the spiritual and physical worlds and also forge a path to knowing our true self.

How is it, then, with the children? We parents and teachers have been handed a sacred task: bringing music to young children. Rudolf Steiner said, "Proper introduction to the musical element is fundamental for a human being to overcome any hindrance that impedes, later in life, a sound development of a will permeated with courage."[1] What did he mean by the "proper" introduction to the musical element? How does the introduction to music affect the development of the will, and what has it to do with courage? I would like to explore these questions.

It is widely acknowledged that in earlier times people sang through their day. They sang in celebration, to heal and soothe, and to accompany their work. Today, most people seldom or never sing. Many feel they are unable to sing well, and so they do not even sing to their children. We need to help the parents of the children in our classes understand the benefits not only to the children, but to themselves and their family, of singing together. Singing not only helps to pass the time while working at the multitude of daily tasks which could otherwise become tedious and dull, but I believe it actually helps us in many other ways. It can bring more joy to any activity, but it also facilitates the actual physical movement, it exercises the lungs and throat and tongue, and strengthens the immune system through an increased sense of well-being.

Rudolf Steiner spoke about the work of the teacher as helping the children learn how to breathe.[2] What better way than by singing? Singing in the classroom is one of the most important tools for working with the breath. Music can guide and carry the breath and metabolic functions in a rhythmic stream or, if not "properly introduced," it can disrupt and throw them into disharmony. Understanding the power of the voice and the effect of tone on the body as well as the surrounding physical space can help us to bring true healing to the world through our work with children.

For young children today who may have little opportunity to see real physical work being done in the home, song is a way to gather them into an activity and can be a real bridge to the actual movement required. For example, during free play in my kindergarten classroom one morning, several children began building a house with large blocks. After a short time the house was knocked down and the play began to deteriorate. One child returned to the pile with a stick and began to "hammer" one block to the next. I began to sing a song while sitting nearby in my rocking chair: "The carpenter hammers nails all day long, to make a house that is sturdy and strong. . ." Like magic, the other children were again drawn to the play and began to help the carpenter. When I stopped singing one little girl said, "Keep singing—we're still working!"

It is easy to see how singing "Come, butter, come. . ." while churning can help facilitate the movement of the arm; it keeps the rhythm so they don't go too fast or too slow. It also helps the children develop self-control while they wait their turn, since they know that we sing the song twice through before the next person has a turn. In my parent-child classes I have found that singing can gently bring parents back to quiet observation when they begin chit-chatting too much while we are baking or sewing. It has become clear to me that singing not only focuses attention on the task at hand, but it can also create form and movement, both within the body and within the physical space of the classroom.

When I began thinking this way, my focus widened and I became more interested in sound itself and how it affects the body and the physical experience of the room itself. How can I use sound to create a healthy space for the children? I have experienced a simple hand-washing activity accompanied by song as a benediction, a sacred moment. What makes it so? It is a combination of sound with the intention of the teacher and the focus of meeting one human being to another in a warm and respectful way. For the children, songs can bring joy to any activity, quiet an upset, help ease transitions, and create a space around them that is healthy and whole. Children have the all-important task of learning how to be human beings on earth at this time, and of learning how to work and interact with others. This work is carried on throughout our lives and I do believe that "the proper introduction to the musical element" can help. I recall reading that Michaela Glöckler, MD, described singing as a way to help generations navigate the time and space that separates them, thus weaving a bridge of love, health, and joy around the world. I have experienced that when we sing with the children we not only give, we receive. This is how we build bridges with one another.

Recently, I heard a news report that described new scientific discoveries about language. It seems that infants interact and learn to communicate through music. The way a mother's voice changes when speaking with her baby, using a sing-song tone and lilting phrasing, is a musical language that all infants respond to and use themselves when they begin vocalizing and learning to speak. Scientists have coined the term "motherese" to refer to this "musical" communication. So in this sense music is our first language.

Unfortunately, many people have lost basic parenting instincts and skills and need help remembering or learning how to create rhythm and warmth at home. One place to start is with music and singing. I have been humbled and honored to observe my own grown daughter as she has created bedtime rituals and daily rhythms at home for her two little ones. She has crafted a lovely bedtime which ends with a simple and beautiful lullaby in the mood of the fifth. It is clear to me how soul-strengthening this is for her children when I witness the two-and-a-half-year-old lovingly putting her dolly to bed with the same song over and over during my visits.

Because little children still have one foot in heaven and one on earth, so to speak, they are truly cared for when we can bring them music in the mood of the fifth. In an article entitled "Mood of the Fifth—The Mood of Childhood," Karen Klaveness states, "Music based on the mood of the fifth feels warm and comforting to the young child. Its light, hovering quality represents his/her connectedness to both heaven and earth and is a powerful force for the preservation of childhood, that uniquely protected state of life which distinguishes human beings and provides a foundation upon which we can embrace our destinies later as adults."[3]

Perhaps we can think of music in the mood of the fifth as creating a space of balance between heaven and earth for the young child, a gentle aid to incarnation, keeping the doorway to heaven open and not letting the children come too quickly to earth. Another expression of this sense of balance is the reference made by Lao Tzu, Chinese philosopher and father of Taoism, to the interval of the fifth as the source of universal harmony between the forces of yin and yang. This quality of balance is even more important today when we are so inundated by electronics and childhood is more at risk than ever before. Perhaps by holding this balanced space for the children in our care we are allowing them to find, in their own time, their right relationship to heaven and earth and a sense of wholeness.

This then brings me back to Rudolf Steiner's words, "Proper introduction to the musical element is fundamental for a human being to overcome any hindrance that impedes, later in life, a sound development of a will permeated with courage." It is the season of Michaelmas as I write this, and an image takes form in my mind. My own way of grasping the underlying truth or quality of Michaelmas is to picture the human being walking forward consciously with feet firmly on the earth while fully aware of the relationship with the heavens, facing with balance and courage whatever comes towards him or her. It seems to me that this is what Steiner is talking about when he speaks of a sound will and courage-filled life, and that we are helping to develop that capacity in the children when we introduce music rightly into their lives.

Being a musician as well as a teacher, I have spent a fair amount of time thinking about sound and how it affects the human body. I remember walking down a residential street as a young mother with my three-year-old daughter. We were enjoying the summer day when all of a sudden there was an angry exclamation from a house across the street. It was as if I had been struck by an invisible, dark fist right in my chest. I physically felt that sound. The form created by that sound shot out at such speed and to such a distance that I was hit by it. It was a horrible feeling—one I have never forgotten. I actually felt a dark presence in the sound and was so affected by it that I still recall it clearly twenty-nine years later. This experience had a powerful impact on me, offering physical evidence that sound has actual form. I felt it. Several years later I found Waldorf education and other people who were interested in questions about the effects of sound. Since then, I have continued to question and search for answers in my own work. I feel that sound has actual forms and that we can work with these forms to balance and heal the environment, the body, and the soul, and in so doing help to heal the world.

In a book titled *Music: Physician for the Times to Come,* there is an article by Cathie Guzzetta which states, "The forms of snowflakes and faces of flowers take on their shape because they are responding to some sound in nature. Likewise it is possible that crystals, plants, and human beings may be, in some way, music that has taken visible form."[4] This is a beautiful picture, but I think it conveys an awesome responsibility—a responsibility not only to protect our environment but to recognize exactly how we are personally affecting the environment. Are we creating a healthy "sound environment" for the children in our care? If sound creates form, what kind of forms are we creating in our classrooms? What forms does mood of the fifth music create? How do these forms affect the physical, soul, and spiritual bodies of ourselves and the children? These are big questions we can all continue to work with.

In my study of the work of Ernst Chladni and Hans Jenny, both pioneers in discovering that sound's vibrations create physical form, I learned that the physical form is affected by lowering or raising the tone just a slight bit—that just a small shift in the tone will begin to erode the harmoniousness and symmetry of the form. I have the sense that were we to see the forms created by mood of the fifth music with our physical eye, we would see rounded, harmonious, flowering patterns, distinct forms at once protective and expansive. In singing the tones purely, beautifully, and on pitch we create clear and consistent forms around the children. This, in turn, reduces stress and strengthens the children. We are building a true sound environment for them to live and play in—we should pay attention to this! In the same way that it is important to surround the children with an ordered and beautiful physical environment, it is just as important to surround them with an ordered and beautiful sound environment.

This is why I feel it is so important for teachers to work on our singing. In our work to create an environment in our classrooms in which the children's senses are nourished and protected, we must remember to work on ourselves. We must deepen our own sense experiences and observe with objectivity our own weaknesses. Not all teachers are natural singers, but it is our responsibility as Waldorf educators to work with the intention of singing as clearly and as in tune as possible. This can seem a big task for some, and I wish to encourage and applaud the efforts of those who recognize singing as a challenge and who work on improving their abilities.

Children today are bombarded by sound at every turn. From the time they wake in the morning until they go to sleep at night they are interrupted in their dream-consciousness by radio, TV, computers, toys, traffic, alarms, sirens, cell phones, loudspeakers, and so on. We can begin to work with sound within our own classrooms with the intention of creating a space that is health-giving and wholesome. This is like giving the children a warm bath—bathing them in the softness and warmth of the human voice every day while they are at school. To work and play with joy as a young child, in an environment which includes the conscious use of harmonious, healing tone, is a true gift for the adult that he or she will one day become. For when as adults we are able to face life's challenges with joy and courage, we in turn give a gift to the world.

Notes

1. Rudolf Steiner, *The Child's Changing Consciousness as the Basis of Pedagogical Practice* (Hudson, NY: Anthroposophic Press, 1996), p. 184.

2. Rudolf Steiner, *Study of Man* (London, Rudolf Steiner Press, 1966), Lecture 1, p. 21.

3. Karen Klaveness, "Mood of the Fifth—The Mood of Childhood," in *The Peridot: A Journal for Creative Educational Ideas*, Vol. 9, No. 2, p. 1.

4. Cathie E. Guzzetta, "Music Therapy: Nursing the Music of the Soul," in *Music: Physician for the Times to Come*, ed. Don Campbell (Quest Books, 1991), p. 149.

Karen Lonsky has worked for many years as a Waldorf early childhood teacher in and around Ithaca, NY. WECAN recently published her book of work songs in the mood of the fifth, A Day Full of Song, and Karen has produced a companion CD as an aid for learning the songs, also available from WECAN. Besides her kindergarten work, Karen is interested in puppetry and handwork, and she and her husband Joe regularly perform with a nine-piece rhythm and blues band, The Destination. Whenever time allows she loves visiting with her grandchildren and singing with them.

This is the Way We Bake our Bread

A Note about Work Songs

NANCY FOSTER

This article, which appeared originally in the Spring/Summer 2007 issue of Gateways, *suggests the importance of allowing children's own inner music or conversation to arise in an environment free of constant music.*

Work songs can be a lovely way to draw children to an activity, to create a mood of enjoyment and purposeful focus, or to discourage excessive chitchat by parents or older children in a group. Baking songs, grinding songs, sawing songs, cleaning songs: all may have a place in a group of children or parents and children.

On the other hand, if over-used, such songs can become a sort of "Waldorf muzak" or "Waldorf elevator music" going on throughout the time of the activity and becoming an unwelcome and invasive background music. This may seem a strong statement indeed, but it is worth considering the possibility that constant singing may prevent children from experiencing their own internal music or rhythm or imaginations as they participate in an activity or play elsewhere in the room.

There has been some study of the spontaneous songs and chants of children at work and play. What may arise naturally from children as an accompaniment to their activity is something at once personal and universal which surely deserves an opportunity for expression. Aside from such spontaneous music or word play, the concentrated silence which can occasionally occur during activity is special in itself and should be permitted its place. Further, the art of conversation—"more refreshing than light," to quote Goethe—has its humble beginnings in early childhood. Teachers sometimes hear wondrous exchanges among children hard at work on their watercolor painting or kneading their dough. Wouldn't it be a pity if such conversational forays were frustrated by constant singing?

It is also good to avoid using songs as a sort of "disguised instruction" to tell children how to do an activity. We strive to teach through imitation. Occasionally a few words of direction will be needed, but these can be offered in a by-the-way, matter-of-fact, brief, and tactful manner to an individual child, perhaps accompanied by physical guidance, in a way that is less consciousness-raising than a song which is sung in a "teaching" manner and almost compels all the children involved to follow its instructions.

Finally, there is a fine line between having a familiar song that becomes associated with a particular activity—which is a healthy thing, such as always having the same song when lighting the candle at circle time—and using a song as a *signal* for something. At clean-up time, for example, it would be fine to have a song to sing now and then during the process, like a happy accompaniment to the activity; but if the teacher starts singing a song as a *signal* that it's time to stop playing and clean up, this creates an abrupt waking-up moment and prevents a more flowing transition in the morning's rhythm.

In summary, work songs can be wonderful for "priming the pump" as an activity begins, and for drawing the mood together if needed along the way, but it is good to leave the children inwardly and outwardly free to find their own rhythm and mood as they work. Many teachers have experienced the magical hum that can arise in a room full of busy children; this hum may be the most beautiful music of all!

Nancy Foster taught children and parents at Acorn Hill Waldorf Kindergarten and Nursery in Silver Spring, MD, USA, for over thirty years. Now retired from teaching, she serves as the Membership Coordinator of the Waldorf Early Childhood Association of North America and teaches in the part-time early childhood teacher education program at Sunbridge Institute.

Singing, Chanting, and Sound-Shape-Making:

Preschoolers Sounding Being in Play

JUDITH K. KIERSTEAD

Judith Kierstead's article is an excerpt, distilled by the author, from her PhD dissertation entitled Listening to the Spontaneous Music-Making of Preschool Children in Play: Living a Pedagogy of Wonder.[1] *Her research was carried out in part through many hours of observation and listening in Waldorf early childhood settings. While her topic is not directly related to mood-of-the-fifth music, her observations are a lively illustration of the consciousness of the young child completely given over in devotion to the experiences of life. They also show us how the child's own "inner music" can be freely expressed in an environment where inner music is not submerged by constant adult speech or background music.*

The singing and chanting and other sound-shape-making of children playing freely in preschool is filled with the wonder of Being-a-child and Beauty that shines through the wisdom of giving-the-gift-of freedom-to-Be to preschoolers. Come listen with me to voices and soundings preschool children make as they freely play indoors and out.

Singing Being-in-the-World

Joshua makes his way across the preschool classroom singing "Good morning!" "Hello!" "Good morning!" Then with one sound straight and another wiggly, he sings seven "Hello"s in a row!

Seven persons neither line up to receive one of his decorated "Hello"s nor stand by as he greets them one by one in passing. Free to *Be*, he adds *another* row of "Hello"s, this one with soundings shaped with a low take-off-tone that stays put and landing tones that change with each "Hello!" Joshua is giving an extraordinary morning greeting!

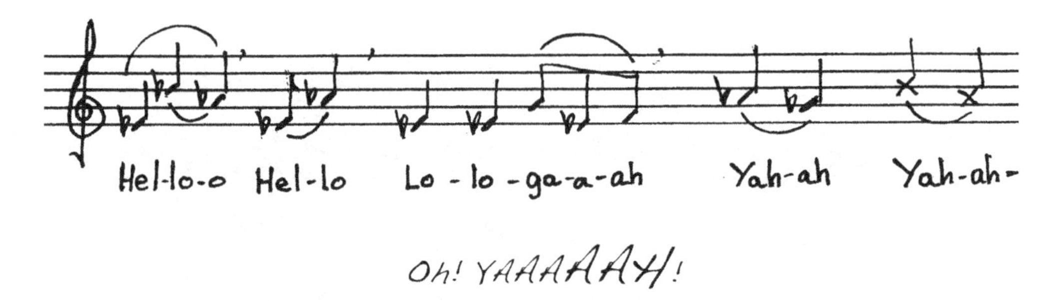

After briefly playing with the "lo" sound, he links a "lo" to a large "Gah!" *and* makes drumming-tones with his running feet: a multi-timbred sound-shape. His next sounds grow into large "Yah!"s and another "Gah!" Clearly, simultaneous largeness in dynamics and movement go together. This "young child is a being of movement"[2] who, with "tremendous trust and confidence" within, *wills*[3] to shape sound at the beginning of his day. The air Joshua breathes "is not neutral or lifeless," for Joshua gives the air life in a stream of "*sound* and *voice*"[4] that moves from a cheery "Good morning!" to a final shouted "Oh! YAAAAAH!" while leaping through the air! Joshua's breathing-out and breathing-in is like the "form of that original Out-In,"[5] the movement of the Breath of all life. Air holds all sounds just as light holds all colors, and in breathings-out and breathings-in, a musical sound-shape is born in preschool.

Chanting Change

Sounds abundant fill the air as preschool children come outside to play. Becky joyfully chants her destination as she heads for the playground gate:

go - - ing to - - the play - - go - - ing to - - the play - -
I'm ground. - I'm ground.

Lydia and Eileen are already there selling their wares:

Fresh crabs for sa-
-ale. . .

they chant in unison as they move together across the grassy area in the center of the playground. Ella is reaching way up, holding onto the handle of the small red bucket of "crabs" Lydia is carrying. Her short legs are *running* beside Lydia's long-leg strides! Later, as Ella walks from the playhouse toward the table under the great tree by the playground gate, she is chanting again. Both the "food" she has on a red sand-sifter plate and the rhythm of her chant have changed.

Fresh cherry pie for sa-
-ale. . .

she chants. What a fine feast—fresh crabs and fresh cherry pie! No feast is planned, however. The children are imagining and chanting-to-be-chanting. Other children are also chanting. Becky chants "Pies" and Patrick chants "for sale" at just the right time, making a sound-tag finish. Like well-trained runners who race in the Olympics and smoothly connect at the right place at exactly the right time, handing over a wand, completing a segment of a race begun by another, Patrick and Becky chant a spontaneous two-person call of "Pies"—"for sale." The two tones that carry children's chanted messages are, indeed, useful and *always* available. This chant-form is fundamental in the voices of children creating sounds in play. The two-tone chant that *always* ends with the low tone a minor third below the other tones has been a faithful carrier of ideas for children all over the world longer than anyone can remember, and it is always present in the sounds voiced by children in communities. Indeed, this chant is "deeply rooted . . . in the world of the young child."[6]

Tree Sharing

Imagine what it might be like to be playing outside and find a tree that you *really* love. That's what happens to Julia one day. She finds a tree on the playground at school that she really, really likes. Oh, how she wants to share her joy with someone. "Who wants to see the tree?" she sings with a row of rather high tones that stay the same until she gets to the most important word: tree. Her voice gives "tree," the very special *thing* she wants to share, a two-tones-close-together sounding at the end of this first part of her tree-song. Singing two tones that work together, her voice bends the "tree-ee"-tones-sounding a little bit downward. The shape she sings is like the firm standing of the tree trunk that holds the long branches steady while the tips of the branches of her tree gently bend in the wind. No one responds immediately to the sound of her voice that carries her question-that-is-an-invitation over the playground. She continues, singing her question again, beginning with the same tone as the first time. Yet, her voice sounds these tones-in-a-row a bit higher as if she is feeling even more eager to share her very special tree. Again a two-tone bending-

"tree-ee" sounds and she returns to her starting tone. There is comfort in going home, even in sound.

Indeed, "The little child is a will being."[7] Julia is determined. She *will* find someone. Who will it be? This time "Who" is a longer sound and "wants" is also stretched, though not quite so much as "Who." Julia *wants* to share the tree with another person. The tones stay the same this time until the "tree-ee"-tones bend again, though covering less distance this time. Her voice sounds tree-tones that are closer together, moving only a half step. An insistence is creeping in through the proximity of the sounds. No one responds, even so. With a final push, like a marathon runner sprinting to the end of the run, her voice contracts her call and with sound moving quickly in tones that double the sprint in sound, the voice the second time moves up ever so slightly. She sings: "Who wants to see? Who wants to see-ee?" "Tree" itself is now missing. "See" carries its weight, and the gentle arch of a would-be-seen tree bends in the sound of the two longer tones that move downward at the very end. The tree gracefully gives way one last time, bending to "see"-ing in sound carried by the voice to a tone a significant half-step higher.

One is changed in experiencing love for a living Other. Julia is repeating and compressing her sounded statement in tones that convey heightened desire to share with an Other something that is important to her. In his classic study *Listening and Voice*, Don Ihde affirms that persons "concerned with the roots of reflection in human experience, must eventually also listen to the *sounds as meaningful.*"[8] The tones and rhythms and musical form Julia is innately shaping in singing spontaneously are, indeed, meaning-full sounds. One grasps meaning present in "*the things themselves,*"[9] in the bending of sounds, in the pace of the movement, in the place of the pitch. The spontaneous music children make while freely playing is meaningful.

Waterfish

Kathryn's light and agile singing-tones dart in and out like the movement of her fish in water. She sings "Twooooooo waterfish," making the sound of the *number* of fish as long as the three-syllable name of the *kind* of creature. "Water" goes by in sprightly tones indeed. What might be chasing the water-word so quickly away? Kathryn sings that the fish she favors is very capable. She speaks not in an ordinary manner, such as "He can do anything!" She sings her perception in a poetic form of language: "all things can he do." Rudolf Steiner says musical and poetic arts harmonize the human being, bringing us into relation with the harmony of the world, whereas "in the sculptural and pictorial realm we look at beauty, and we live it; in the musical realm we ourselves become beauty."[10]

After pointing with high tones to "two waterfish," Kathryn, with seemingly thoughtful discretion, voices her preference for one fish over the other, sounding lower tones. As she gives voice to "all things," the weighty sound of the minor third is called upon to ground "he can do" as her voice carries the ability of her waterfish forward realistically. The sound of the two ending tones, only one-half step apart, are close to whole-step-soundness. What might her "fav'rite" waterfish be striving for within? Might a young child have an inner sense of balance and propriety—or a seeming need to be "perfect," like an adult says? The sound of three tones that take two full upward musical steps is a sound with certainty. Three tones that take a large step and then only half of one say, "Are you sure?"

> *The very idea of "perfection" can convey a sense of coldness, of rigidity, of fixedness. Striving, however, brings warmth and movement, which can encourage our children and provide a wonderful example of the essence of what it is to be a human being: the capacity to grow and change, to learn, to exert ourselves for the sake of others. Such honest, consistent striving is . . . one of the greatest gifts we can offer our children.*[11]

Kathryn is playing freely, sounding her voice, singing her *Be-ing*.

Puddle-Stepping

On a wet no-longer-raining morning, Jonathan, Leif, and James find a welcoming rain-puddle at the right front corner of the school building. "Splish! Splash! Splish! Splash!" sings Jonathan alongside Leif and Connor, who also are splashing. Neighboring tones sound Jonathan's first "Splish! Splash!" and the so-often-present minor third sound returns with a "Splash!" to the very sound Jonathan started on. Jonathan made a "Splish! Splash!" circle with the sound of his voice. Then, four times in a row Jonathan calls "Splash! Splash! Splash! Splash!" The "Splishes!" are gone! What might let "Splash!" be all on its own now? Perhaps *making* splashes gives the "Splash!"-sound staying-power.

Three boys hear the sound made by their feet hitting first the water surface and then the sidewalk. They see myriad water-shapes fly up, out, and down again all around and on them all. They feel the wetness of rain and consequent coldness. The three boys splash-and-say-"Splash!" together, all at the same time. "Splash!" "SPLASH!" and another "SSPLAAAASH!" What fun it is to make sooooo much water splash all at once AND make sounds that match the splashing! Loud, LOUDER, and LOUDER they are! These puddle-splashers are living an experience in a "way of knowledge" that lets them be "intimate participants in life."[12] The "phenomena of universal nature" are whispering to them deep within and, in response, they are making and singing "Splish!"-ings" and "Splash!"-ings. Indeed, they are filled with a zest for life imparted by Mother Nature herself.

The teacher allows this play, knowing that the children's experience is laying a foundation for "studying the physical effects of wind, clouds, rain, and sun."[13] Splashing in the rain-puddle makes "knowledge a complete human experience."[14] When the time is right, Teacher calls softly, "Come, please." The boys *will*ed to get wet; now they *will* to leave the wetness. Such self-educating of their will in preschool will bring them freedom-to-be in the years to come. As the boys begin their trek back into the school, Jonathan sings:

He lifts his foot up high in front of his bright yellow macintosh—and his boot falls off! "Oh! My gosh! My sock is wet!" he exclaims in surprise. "My sock is wet!" "My sock is wet, too!" echo Conner and Leif. Teacher and three contented, very wet boys make their way through the door to warmth and dryness.

The human spirit gives voice to Be-ing. With singing and chanting and sound-shape-making children affirm self and nurture relationships, creating community. Wonder shines from within the child—and in the hearts of those who listen nearby. The soundings of voices in free play at preschool are roots to be welcomed and watered. Listen . . . Listen . . . Listen . . .

Notes

1. Judith K. Kierstead, *Listening to the spontaneous music-making of preschool children in play: Living a pedagogy of wonder* (College Park, MD: University of Maryland College Park, 2006). http://hdl.handle.net/1903/41842

2. Nancy Foster (ed.). *Dancing as We Sing: An Acorn Hill Anthology of Songs, Verses, and Stories for Children, Vol. 2* (Silver Spring, MD: Acorn Hill Waldorf Kindergarten & Nursery, 1999), p. 4.

3. Joop Van Dam, "Understanding imitation through a deeper look at human development," in Susan Howard (ed.), *The Developing Child: The First Seven Years* (Spring Valley, NY: Waldorf Early Childhood Association of North America, 2004), p. 101.

4. D. Ihde, *Listening and Voice: A Phenomenology of Sound* (Athens: Ohio University Press.1976), p. 3.

5. Herbert Whone, "Music, the way of return," in *Parabola: Myth and the quest for meaning*, 5 (2) 2001, p. 9.

6. Donald Pond, *Melody Observed in Early Childhood and How to Use It Creatively* (Unpublished manuscript, Donald Pond Archives, Special Collections in Music, University of Maryland College Park, 1981), p. 5.

7. Van Dam, op. cit., p. 101.

8. Ihde, op. cit., p. 4.

9. E. Husserl, *The Phenomenology of Internal Time-Consciousness* (Bloomington: Indiana University Press, 1911/1980), p. 116.

10. Rudolf Steiner, *Rhythms of learning: What Waldorf Education Offers Children, Parents & Teachers / Selected Lectures by Rudolf Steiner*, Roberto Trostli, ed. (Great Barrington, MA: Anthroposophic Press, 1998), p. 297.

11. Nancy Foster, *In a Nutshell: Dialogues with Parents at Acorn Hill, a Waldorf Kindergarten* (Silver Spring, MD: Acorn Hill Waldorf Kindergarten & Nursery, 2005), p. 91.

12. Rudolf Steiner, *The Kingdom of Childhood* (Hudson, NY: Anthroposophic Press, 1995), p. 99.

13. John Fentress Gardner, *Education in Search of the Spirit* (Hudson, NY: Anthroposophic Press, 1996), p. 99.

14. Ibid., p. 99.

Judith Kierstead began teaching music classes for preschool children while completing her undergraduate studies at the University of Michigan. Drawn to the varied interests and spontaneous soundings of young children, she assisted with the archiving of materials in Special Collections in Music at the University of Maryland that confirmed her own listening experience, and received her PhD from The University of Maryland College Park in 2006. During her doctoral study, a Waldorf school child named her "The Listener Lady." She now shares her work and experience with students in Fine Arts college courses.

“If music be the food of love, play on”

SALLY SCHWEIZER

This article appeared originally in Kindling, *the Steiner/Waldorf early years journal in the United Kingdom, and is reprinted with the author’s kind permission. The author’s great joy in music and in young children speaks clearly through her chosen title (a quotation from a Shakespeare play,* Twelfth Night*), as well in as the rich contents of her article.*

Overture

Pantomime, circus, children’s concert: painful amplified speech and music. “It’s too noisy!” says a little child.

Children are suffering in the hearing realm. I hope to show how one can counteract much of this with a musical environment. Our gestures can speak with musicality and even the harmonious arrangement of a room is like beautiful music. The human voice is the greatest instrument of all. Imbuing it with conscious but simple artistry is a precious image for children.

Society has become immune to background music, loud or soft. Much recorded singing is actually shouting. Not only the electronic nature or poor quality of music many children hear is damaging, but the *volume.* An audiologist told me that an increasing number of young people manifest reduced hearing also from *an accumulation of noise.* This affects the social, heart realm. What was once intolerable has become acceptable; silence is unwelcome. The frequent repetition in some pop music is without variation or breath. But songs on the knee and circle time repetitions are living, breathing.

A Musical Environment

Hearts thrive and glow to beautiful live music, while repetition, clarity and simplicity offer sustenance to breathing, circulation and life. Musical forces lead to reverence and the child’s spiritual nature is set free in singing. We can make any song or verse a play of wonderful impressions. Remembering that many children do not have enough experience of a live human voice makes it imperative for teachers to find every opportunity for good speech and song. Children cannot think abstractly, so they need to see, hear, or touch what is going on.

The Lower Senses and Music

Touch is enhanced by *playing an instrument* and *harmonious vibrations.* We are touched by music, warmed or repelled by it. With the experience of music being part of the child's wholeness of being, it is not hard to understand that loud, jerky or violent music may hurt, as it is drunk in through the very skin.

Movement is fed by *rhythm*, giving a delicate sense or an aggressive one, an energetic mood or a peaceful one. Simple, flowing rhythms are helpful.

Life: Song immediately springs to mind here. Its type and quality are of great influence. Gentle and calming, joyful and fun, quick and lively or slow and deep: such moods affect the soul and the sense of life.

Balance and *melody* seem obvious partners. Cheerful, lively circle time tunes followed by quiet, gentle ones and vice versa bring balance. "Chaos" to "calm" feeds the child's soul. Historically, melody came before rhythm, so we don't need to make the beat too strong. Concentrate on flowing melodies. Variations of loud and quiet, fast and slow, up and down or high and low are nourishing.

Hearing, Beat and Rhythm

The quality of listening is diminishing in children, who hear with their whole body. Sensitivity generally is diminishing, so loudness has to be increased to gain the same effect. Rhythm and beat influence the circulatory and respiratory systems. If there is barely a melody to balance it, one can feel oppressed by rhythm slower than the heartbeat, or excited if faster. In the latter, an ecstatic state can be induced. Such music goes through the digestive system, desensitizing it, penetrating right through to the will and overburdening the nervous system. It is easy to see the detrimental effect on life forces and the soul.

In much education children hear and sing to recorded music, but our early childhood settings provide a haven of live music. Our awareness of balance helps us to know how we should act when play becomes so noisy that a child says "it's too loud." Is there a danger of stressing children when we sing or hum too long? Unnecessary whispering stresses the child too!

The unborn child hears in the womb. It follows that mothers who listen to harmonious music may help the child. It is best if she makes or sings it herself! The first rhythm a baby is likely to hear is three beats in a bar (measure)—the swinging, rocking of the lullaby (3/8 or 6/8) and skipping or galloping. Depending on the tempo (speed), the simple beat of 2/4 and 4/4 can be slow and reverent or quick and down-to-earth, as in trotting. It is better generally to avoid syncopated rhythms, where the beat is turned inside out, as it were. One can vary the tempo within a song, but it should be the same variation when repeated. Is one's pace fast enough for the older children not to be bored, yet slow enough for the younger ones to follow? It will inevitably have to be a mixture of both. Our musical feeling should help in measuring our tempo!

More about Movement

We speak of being moved by music. It can make us tremble or clasp our hands, dance for joy or weep. In the child the movement of music also affects body and soul. Electronic music is produced through electrical impulses so there is no true resonation. How does a child move to which kind of music? Tuneful, harmonious songs encourage rounded, balanced gesture. Jerky, loud pop music is imitated in ugly, inharmonious movement.

"Emotion" means "out of movement." Our emotions are movements in heart and soul, expressed in body language. Such complementary activity must illustrate what a gift it is for the little child, active mainly in the physical body, to find adults gracing their song and verse with movement, from knee rhymes to pictorial images in songs. Gesture speaks to children long before words; they understand body language before that of the tongue. So, we can enliven our words by doing the action expressed immediately before the spoken or sung language. This takes skill and one can never refine it enough. No one needs to study art or music to feel their way into such skill. These talents of artistic musicality or musical artistry are latent in everyone.

Pentatonic and Fifth Tuning

In some parts of the world natural harmonic overtones are produced in song or string and wind instruments, different from the "well-tempered" scales we use today. Intervals of a fifth are the most harmonious of all, corresponding to the open nature of the young child. The pentatonic scale is composed of fifths. Young children sing a double fifth effortlessly whereas we want to revert to an octave.

In third grade in Waldorf education, children meet the polarity of major and minor: adding semitones (two notes next to each other) to make the interval of a third. This leads to settling down to a tonic or "home" note, and creates bright and happy or sad and melancholy moods. We avoid exposing young children to strong feelings and intellectual activity in order to concentrate on the development of their physical body, so we offer songs without semitones in the *pentatonic* mode, which is used all over the world in folk music.

There are many such pieces which actually give a feeling of major or minor. Yet the *fifth mood* within the pentatonic is like a hovering, starting and ending anywhere, not belonging or leading somewhere particular. The scale is the same but the quality is different. The fifth tuning gives *no mood*, leaving the child's feelings free. Because of this, the notes can be harmoniously mixed. However, as balance is the essence of all things, children also can be immersed in the riches of nursery rhymes and folk tunes from their own culture.

In this pentatonic song, there is an open feeling of the "fifth mood," as you do not want to go back to a "home" or "tonic" note. You can create many tunes on just two or three notes.

The moon shines clear as silver, the sun shines bright as gold.
And they are very lovely, and very, very old.
God hung them up as lanterns, for all beneath the sky,
And nobody can blow them out, for they are up too high.

Please repeat songs and verses at least three times. If they are filled with musicality and pictorial gestures, not even six-year-olds will get bored. They need such rhythm as food to build up their life forces.

Pitch

This is where music is "placed." It is helpful for the child to experience the constancy of a tune which stays in the same place. So striving to keep the same pitch throughout a song helps the children to follow. An assistant can help in keeping level by playing the first note of each verse on a glockenspiel. Many adults struggle to sing high enough for children, yet in keeping their voice up, they match the high voice of the young. Men can practice singing an octave below the children's natural range. It can be done!

I do not believe that people can never sing in tune. Ask someone to help you. Practice fifths first, as they can provide a basis for the other notes. "Twinkle twinkle little star" begins with fifths, so if you can manage that, you are well on your way. Otherwise try singing up and down the scale, *1,2,3,4,5–5,4,3,2,1* or conjure a little phrase: "Please go up the hill/Come down if you will." Children become confused when their teacher wanders about the tune and may not sing at all, so it is really good to get help. I have worked successfully with students who were sure they couldn't do it.

Singing

The voice is the infant's first toy. It is delightful to listen to babies' joyful operatic rehearsal, providing their own entertainment. People talk to them in a naturally sing-song way. "How are /You, my /Dar-Ling/ Have you just /Wo-ken /Up?" Chanting the story in kindergarten helps the whole group if someone is upset.

It is a real shame that many think babies and children need background music, for they "'sing" without any help from us. One may actually inadvertently provide such diversion in the setting by singing or humming much of the morning to no real purpose. Is this not background noise, just as when a teacher talks much of the time? Children tend then not to listen or respond. We like singing a "sailor's shanty" to help an activity along, yet it should be focused, not endless. We all need an interval, a moment to breathe out. Tidying up, painting, whatever the song is: just a few times is enough, maybe repeated after a while.

We are so used to music being turned on and off or faded in and out! When we have to see to something or sort out a problem in circle time, we may stop in the middle of a tune, thereby inadvertently interrupting the children's dream world. It is better to continue it to the end while seeing to the nosebleed, spilt paint or disruptive child.

A hurt knee is soothed with a simple song, a rowdy playtime transformed with a focused melody on two or three notes. Is it necessary always to sing to lead the children from one place to another, for instance from the cloakroom to the story circle? *Out of rhythm and imitation of your gesture* they will do it anyway. How lovely to burst into song on a walk, or take a stick or two to play the "flute" or "violin"! Your children will join in lustily because it is special.

With small children it is essential to sound clear notes, and the easier the song, the more the children can imitate. We want them to sing in tune, and some do so when they first come to kindergarten, but all should be able to do it when they leave for school. It is essential for the teacher to be able to at least read if not write simple music.

The Voice

Clear enunciation is vital. One might be inadvertently a bit too quiet or loud, a touch sharp or sloppy. It is excellent if the teacher's voice is kept for those who need to hear it, not calling across the room unnecessarily, for instance. A baby has the potential to speak any language until settling on the mother tongue. We understand from Rudolf Steiner that the mother tongue feeds the child's life forces and that speech shapes the child's bones and organs. As children learn to speak also through lip reading, it is essential that they see people speaking well. Movement in the mouth (small motor skill) is connected to the whole body; the sounds we make reverberate in our whole being and into that of the child. It is helpful to work on this our instrument, increasing its clarity, flexibility and artistic, expressive qualities.

One can recognize a language just through its tones, as every tongue has its own "music." I liked students from abroad to do a circle or story in their own language, for this was a true model, rather than English with a foreign accent.

The Lyre

The seven-stringed *lyre* or *children's harp* is the classic instrument of our early childhood education. Holding it upright like an angel's wing with the highest strings closest to the heart, draw your fingers across ("glissando") up and down. The thumb is not used. For individual notes, keeping the fingers upright and fairly straight, stroke (gently pull) rather than pluck each string. You can control the finger by stopping it on the next-door string, though I prefer to leave it free as the *gesture* is more open and lyre-like, as if letting the sound continue reverberating. For a puppet show or story, repeat the same phrases at beginning and end, and perhaps accompany a song or two in between. I advise that only adults play the lyre as a good example, and the children should dream rather than be active. Please play loudly enough for them to hear, for straining to listen awakens them. Children like to take the lyre for their playtime puppet shows, but it must be replaced when no longer wanted and on no account left on the floor. They should know how to play it if they observe their teacher using it properly. Use it also for eurythmy.

Tuning the Lyre

Be very careful not to tighten the tuning key too far too quickly, or you will need to run to the music shop for another string! You can buy lyre strings but guitar strings are adequate. Laying the lyre flat on your knee or in its box, use a tuning fork to tune the lyre's middle string a′. Pluck the string repeatedly with the right hand while turning the key with the left. You will hear the note changing while adjusting it up (tighter) or down (looser). Then tune a′ with bottom d′, a fifth, until they vibrate in harmony. Follow with a′ to top e″ a fifth above. Tune this e″ with octave e′ below and bottom d′ with octave d″ above. The last intervals of a fifth are top d″ to g′ and bottom e′ to b′.

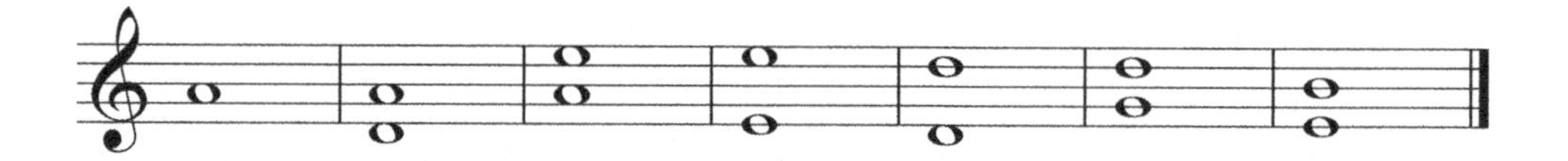

Please check the lyre every time you play and retune if need be. If you still find tuning difficult, ask a friend, parent or colleague to help you learn. *There is absolutely no point in playing it out of tune.* The notes will not move together harmoniously and the children will not be helped to sing cleanly.

Other Tone Pictures

Composers and teachers choose diverse instruments for their different qualities. The lyre is so versatile that it can be used for any image, from birds flying glissando to clumsy dwarfs on two low notes. For young children I prefer to keep *sound quality* distinct, for example not mixing the lyre with other instruments, and using those of metal separately from wooden ones. It depends what tone image you want.

The metal *glockenspiel* with its crystalline, clear sound must be hit gently, otherwise it is painful. The wooden *xylophone* has a quite different quality. I suggest only adults using these instruments. Use *rhythm sticks, rattles, coconut shells, a triangle, chime bars, tiny finger cymbals* for accompanying eurythmy or ringtime.

You can take *metal wind chimes* apart, hang them from thin copper wire and strike then with chopsticks. Play separated *bamboo* ones, hung from string, with small sticks. Make "*tubular bells*" from brass curtain rods hung on nylon thread and hit with rubber drum sticks. Saw one to about 30 cm. Strike it to check the note, then file the end until it is correct. Continue with ever-longer ones.

A tiny *bell* represents something exquisite. Hang them round the neck on thin ribbon for certain circle times, and make a "secret" when they are not needed by tucking them into the collar (playful discipline!). They look pretty hung in a rainbow on a branch of tiny hooks. Let the children take the one they want for a particular circle time. Children enjoy bigger bells for playtime and wearing them on ribbons round the wrist for the maypole.

You can create an "orchestra" with percussion instruments during circle time. For a heavenly sound such as stars, a journey across the sky, or a snowy scene, I use *metal* instruments. You might take *wooden* ones or *seed pods* for earthy, clumsy or hardened sounds, portraying a bear, witch or bad dwarf. With the instruments prepared in baskets on a big table, move over at the appropriate moment to take one and play a very simple repetitive rhythm. The children will imitate and move about freely for a few minutes, creating a wonderful picture in sound. Then lay yours back, the children following and continue the circle. I would only do it once in a circle, avoiding all instruction.

The children did not often use percussion otherwise apart from their own creations or for special occasions. Some kindergartens have percussion instruments including a glockenspiel for creative playtime but I advise against it. The noise is disturbing and children may not play them properly.

The piano is not needed in our kindergartens because of its well-tempered nature and defined keys. It is not wrong to play the piano to children! It is just that we offer simpler music in our settings. My uncle, Benjamin Britten, at age two, his head full of golden curls, used to say "Dear pay pano," thus driving his older (very talented) brother from the piano because his mother would give in to this very gifted child who could already play little tunes.

Instrument Care

Please create a good habit of children and adults washing and drying hands before playing anything. You don't want sticky instruments, especially not strings. Little bags for small instruments and baskets for several of the same larger ones are attractive. The lyre should be wrapped in silk and/or felt and maybe kept in a box. Never leave it uncovered, near a radiator, or on a windowsill as the strings go out of tune quickly and it could crack.

Eurythmy

You can support your eurythmist by playing an instrument to match the gestures. Our excellent eurythmist, Thea Kaesbach, joined us for our initial three circle verses. I melted into the background to make music while she continued. I only played when she was not singing or speaking. Examples: a lyre tune for birds flying; rhythm sticks for a horse trotting; finger cymbals or triangle for the blacksmith; lyre fifths up and down for balancing across a bridge. As she spoke the final verse, I slipped into the circle with the lyre to play a few fifths upwards, a′ to e″. Then we all sat quietly for a few minutes.

Parental Musical Involvement

It is joyful to invite parents to help with music. Any teacher can do it with a little courage, even the most quiet amongst us. Whatever you do seems miraculous for the children. Gradually you won't mind singing in front of others. We used to practice a song or two for the forthcoming festival at the parents' evening. They really enjoyed this as they could sing it with their children. At a festival or the maypole, parents like to play a recorder, guitar, flute or a lyre or bell that you give them. Assistants are a wonderful help. To avoid a "show" attitude, prepare parents to have no photos, videos, or applause. Once a parent demonstrated his bassoon to my kindergarten children. In the next-door group, a child apparently said, "Shhhh, everyone, Sally's playing her lyre."

The Maypole

All over the world, children love to dance to folk music, twirling, stamping and clapping, moved by melody and rhythm. It is good to move rhythmically but not too strongly with young children. Rhythm is very active *within* until seven, so one cannot expect them to be rhythmical yet. It is difficult to sing while dancing, so one can begin by walking while singing round the maypole. Crowned with fresh flowers and with bells round our wrists, we danced to my fiddle and whatever parents and assistants could play, with ribbons tied to the instruments! I think the maypole is lovely in a lightly organized, happy-go-lucky atmosphere. There is another aspect to song and dance with the young: it must enhance the life forces of the adults as well.

Singing Games

Movement in a ring creates fairy-tale images. First is simply a circle, reflecting oneness, eternity. Birth is reflected in falling to the ground. Standing in the center, the child is alone but still held by the group ("The farmer in the dell"). The circle turning towards the outside and back ("Water, Water, Wallflower"), is like taking a peep at the new seven-year-old consciousness. Traveling in and out through archways made by the group ("In and out the dusty bluebells") symbolizes flowing between the first two stages of childhood between six and seven. The second stage of childhood is characterized by going round the outside of the circle alone ("I sent a letter to my love"). Two lines facing each other reflects questions and answers, appropriate for school children ("Allygaloo"). A line weaving in and out with a head and a tail (leader) pictures thinking. So one must be careful in choosing circle games, in order to be appropriate to the age of the children. Steiner spoke of only being able to work with what is in front of us in the early years, that is, the physical body.

Any movement of the kindergarten circle should follow the same clockwise direction (as plants grow, or the way the sun appears to move round the earth). Turning to counter-clockwise (widdershins or the witches' way) is an awakening change. It becomes a stable, unthinking rhythm to the child always to move clockwise. The exception is of course maypole dancing as the ribbons have to be untied!

This game for the younger child is similar to "Ring-a-ring-a-roses," picturing birth, incarnation. Being egoists, children should never have to hold hands if they don't want to.

These songs are pleasing also for parent and child groups.

(Shake hands, touch feet, sit down, stand up etc.)

As individualizing by choosing a child is not appropriate for children under six, one can enjoy simple circle games where several go into the center at once or everyone does the same thing.

"Rosy Apple," "Oats and Beans," and other such games require a single part, yet why not several children as the groom, prince or whoever? More then have a turn and they are not made self-conscious. They should not be awake to the fact that there is only one part in the song. Boy or girl is irrelevant. I used to say "I wonder who is going to be the prince," and wait a moment while some came into the circle of their unconscious, free will, girls and boys. In this way, younger children may drift in as well, and one can help a little when they need a bride, putting two together. It may become a bit of a quiet muddle but who cares? We can hum it once round in the circle and then do it again!

Rosy apple, mellow pear,
Bunch of roses she shall wear,
Gold and silver by her side,
I know who shall be my bride.
[Circle round, children choose brides.]

Take her by the lily-white hand,
Lead her o'er the water.
[Lead brides in and out of arches made by the rest of the group.]
Give her kisses, one two three,
She's a lady's daughter.
[Dance together, no kisses necessary!]

For musicality, vary your speaking pitch within the lines of this verse, supported by wandering about:

Old John Muddlecombe has lost his cap.
He couldn't find it anywhere, the poor old chap.
He walked down the High Street and everybody said:
Silly John Muddlecombe, you've got it on your head!

This verse is just so English. And I don't shy away from saying "silly," although I would not say it to a child.

An action game for breathing follows. Recite it slowly, then speed up with variation in pitch.

Roly, poly, ever so slowly

With low voice, wind hands round each other more and more slowly, with pregnant pause. . .

Whirly, whirly gig!

With high voice, wind hands round each other really fast and hide them behind the back on "gig."

Almost every song or rhyme offers an opportunity for a moment of suspension and silence, something which many children experience but little in their lives. Holding back is not part of modern vocabulary. Ending circle or eurythmy time by sitting in silence for a few minutes brings harmony to soul and life, helping to establish the spiritual nature in the child instead of its flowing away. Through our musical environment, let us help children to retain their beautiful awe-inspired innocence.

Recapitulation

- Beautiful music lifts us into another sphere.
- A simple musical environment enriches the whole life of the child.
- Involve parents in musical activities.
- Develop the courage to speak with them about electronic music and speech.
- Practice enunciation, musical speech and singing in tune.
- Accompany eurythmy with music.
- Balance pentatonic and mood-of-the-fifth music with our rich cultural heritage of children's tunes.
- Choose songs and verse with linguistic musicality in mind.
- Keep lyres tuned and care for instruments.
- Balance fun and joy with seriousness and reverence.
- Fill all musical activity with grace, movement, and gesture.

Coda

What is more delightful than listening to a familiar song on the knee of a loved one? Comforting, uplifting, simple, and wonder-full. If one takes this as the sound basis in music for young children, one does not need to stray very far to find everything appropriate for their musical education.

Fill your home and early childhood group with simple music! Through an all-embracing musical environment we can help lift up the children's souls to the spirit of the world. Our belief that in their simple being they cannot yet control what they do gives us the strength and courage to approach them in a gesture of all-embracing warmth and love. This overrides all troubles, for it permeates all we do and fills their souls. Rudolf Steiner said: "Love is the devotion to the destiny of the one loved."

Author's Note

Tunes are can be played on the pentatonic lyre or pipe; for tunes in D or G major keys, omit notes when necessary while still singing them. I do not know the composers of the tunes—lost in the mists of time—and apologize for not acknowledging them.

Sally Schweizer has been immersed in music from babyhood. As goddaughter of Peter Pears and niece of Benjamin Britten, she was much influenced by many great artists. She gained Distinction in her music as main subject finals in teacher training, but decided not to pursue it professionally. She played the treble viol with an early music group for some years, and took up the Celtic harp at age fifty. She still sings, plays recorder, violin, piano, and harp. She recently retired after many years of teacher training and forty years of working with children, the last nineteen of which were at Michael Hall School in Forest Row, England.

Musical Instruments in the Classroom?

NANCY FOSTER

This brief article was first published in the book In a Nutshell: Dialogues with Parents at Acorn Hill, a Waldorf Kindergarten, *to address a question from a parent.*

Question: Could you address the question of musical instruments in the classroom? I notice that the lyre is the only instrument used by the teacher. Wouldn't it be good for the children to have a broader experience? And what about rhythm instruments for the children? Many preschools have these available, and I haven't seen this at Acorn Hill.

Answer: The young child's sense of hearing, like the other senses, is still delicate and impressionable, and it is our responsibility both to protect and to nurture this very important sense, which is one of the young child's gateways to the world.

In a subtle way, we learn something about the quality, the essence, of whatever substance is producing a sound. Have you ever tapped a bowl with your fingernail in an effort to determine whether it is made of porcelain, or look-alike plastic, or glass? This is just one example of what our hearing can tell us.

In bringing an infant into the world, we want most of all to welcome him or her into the realm of human beings—into the family, and then gradually into the wider world of friends and community. Thus it follows that at first the most important sounds are human sounds: gentle speaking and singing. The human voice could be said to be the first musical instrument, and for the early years of life it remains the most important instrument for the child both to hear and to "play." How fortunate is the child whose parents sing at home. Never mind if the voice is not beautiful; because it expresses the inner qualities of love and warmth, it is a great gift to the child. In the Waldorf early childhood classroom, we use the voice with care and love, and singing is heard often during the morning.

Another important "musical instrument" is the human body. At circle time we may clap, pat our legs, stamp our feet, or drum our fingertips on the floor to create sounds. Older children love to practice snapping their fingers, listening closely for that certain sound. During playtime, children can often be seen and heard creating sounds with the objects around them—tapping or pounding stones together, or beating a stump with a stick. They may also use play materials as imaginary instruments; one boy in my class frequently sought out a particular curved length of wood which he liked to use as a saxophone. This always gave him great satisfaction—and the rest of us did not have to endure the actual sound of a saxophone at close quarters!

Because we prefer to offer the children open-ended play materials—that is, materials which can be used in many different ways, according to the child's needs of the moment—we also do not provide many of the traditional rhythm toys. However, some teachers do have bells, gourds, perhaps a drum or pentatonic xylophone available in the classroom. These allow the children further opportunities to explore sound. It is important that these instruments produce a good quality sound and, in the case of the xylophone, that the notes are in tune. The children may play freely with these instruments, as long as they treat them with appropriate care and the sounds do not become disruptive to the mood of the classroom. In these early years, the children are not asked to play these instruments in a particular rhythm, and in my class I do not use rhythm instruments during circle time, since I feel it is better for the children to find their own way into the world of rhythm rather than having the adult sense of rhythm imposed on them in this way.

Teachers use the lyre, or children's harp, in the classroom because of the gentle purity of tone. Influenced by its soft sound, the children's sense of hearing is heightened and becomes attuned to tone quality and pitch. When I taught a mixed-age class, I would sometimes allow the children to hold and play the lyre, showing them how to make the "wind" by stroking their fingers over the strings. The children found this a magical experience, and I learned much about the children as I watched their approach to the instrument. Some were timid, almost afraid to make a sound, some tried to produce tones as loudly as possible, others seemed to have an innate sense for the gesture which would produce a harmonious "wind" sound.

Of course children's experiences in the world of music are not limited to their hours at school, and it would not be realistic to expect that they would never hear any other kind of music. In our family, for example, my husband is a professional musician and I also played an instrument, so our children grew up surrounded with classical music. One day, many years ago, I decided to take my cello to school and play for the children in my class, thinking this would be a good experience for them. As it turned out, this was something I never repeated. The cello seemed so out of place in the classroom, so large and so loud; and what was Mrs. Foster doing playing that thing?! It was completely out of context.

In the Waldorf primary years the children are introduced to other instruments, and their experiences are broadened. In the early childhood years, we can lay the foundation for these experiences through allowing the children plenty of opportunity to hear and use the singing voice and to explore the world of sound freely through play. We can also take care that as parents we think carefully about the sounds and styles of music to which we expose our children. Just as we protect our children from stories which are too powerful for their stage of development, we should be conscious of protecting them from music which may be fine for adults but which is over-stimulating or overpowering for the more delicate senses of the young child. If we can preserve, protect, and nourish the sense of hearing from the earliest years of a child's life, we will do much to ensure that he or she will have the capacity to live fully in the world of sound and music throughout the rest of life.

Nancy Foster taught children and parents at Acorn Hill Waldorf Kindergarten and Nursery in Silver Spring, MD, USA, for over thirty years. Now retired from teaching, she serves as the Membership Coordinator of the Waldorf Early Childhood Association of North America and teaches in the part-time early childhood teacher education program at Sunbridge Institute.

What Is the "Right Thing" for the Child?

ESTELLE BRYER

Writing out of the wisdom of her many years of experience with children, Estelle Bryer warns against dogmatism in regard to music and young children, reminding us, "Each child is a riddle that we have to solve and there are no dogmatic answers."

We anthroposophists can sometimes have blinkers on and become too dogmatic when it comes to looking at what is "the right thing" for the child. There are three lessons from my very long career as Waldorf kindergarten teacher, eurythmy therapist, and puppeteer that I would like to share with you.

The kalimba is an African musical instrument made of large nails beaten flat and set into wood at the one end. It is small (about five inches by four inches), is held between the hands and played with the thumbs.

About forty years ago I was fortunate enough to visit a wonderful Englishman who was a well-known expert in African tribal music. On his isolated farm he developed the kalimba as well as other instruments for commercial use in order to promote African music.

The notes of his electronically-tuned kalimbas were so pure that I thought that pentatonic ones would be wonderful in the kindergarten. Together, after many trials we developed one easy for a child to hold and play. The sample was very well accepted and played by the children. I got each parent to get their child one for Christmas and when we played our instruments together it sounded like a soft musical waterfall—just wonderful. However. . . playing just with the thumbs? What effect would that have on their development?

Once, while at an international kindergarten conference in Hanover, I asked Dr. Knierim, an expert on instruments for the kindergarten, about this and showed him the kalimba. He said he would think about it. I soon after showed it to Dr. Lein Mees who was one of the first anthroposophical doctors in Holland and also a musician. He just laughed and said, "Why must we always analyze everything? Why can't we just let the children have a little fun?" I have never forgotten this.

I am also a puppeteer and have been so for over forty years. I have very many puppets of all kinds (except marionettes with many strings!). My favorites are glove puppets. They are all "Waldorf style" except for my Zuzu. She is a glove-puppet monkey with a gorgeous little mobile plastic face. I found her "by chance" and when I looked into her eyes we spoke to each other. She has been my favorite ever since.

I still perform at least sixty times a year and always use Zuzu beforehand. She is my medium through which I tell stories at old-age homes and also for therapy at a childrens' hospital. Zuzu is by far everyone's favorite and all the children love her the most. They even stop me in the street to ask about her. It's the *tangible love* between us that is the important factor and it is *what lives between* that works so deeply into the life forces of the child. She does not speak but I understand and interpret her, and this is also part of her charm.

Lastly: If someone asked me if a three- or four-year-old child could go to symphony concert rehearsals I would certainly raise my eyebrows! Think of the harm to their sense of hearing! Expect them to sit still for so long? Never! In an article in *Anthroposophy Worldwide* (June 2006), "Music as a Cosmic Force," I read that "even in the womb the human ear is already important; our early hearing experiences influence our later life," and this made me think of my grandson.

My youngest daughter and son-in-law are musicians. My daughter played in the symphony orchestra until her eighth month of pregnancy, then went to all the rehearsals and concerts until my grandson was born. When he was three years old and she was in the orchestra again she would take him with her to rehearsals. There I would watch him sit absolutely still with his little hand keeping perfect time to the music through an entire concerto.

He is now twenty-two, a gifted composer and musician, studying music at the university of San Francisco.

I know that this is an exceptional case, but it was a good example for me also as a eurythmy therapist for it made me realize that one must investigate every child thoroughly, including the family background, before giving advice or making judgments. Each child is a riddle that we have to solve, and there are no dogmatic answers.

As an octogenarian, Estelle Bryer still tells stories to adults and children, lectures, and gives puppet workshops to students in Cape Town. She is the author of Movement for the Young Child: A Handbook for Eurythmists and Kindergarten Teachers *(WECAN, 2011) and* The Rainbow Puppet Theatre Book: Fourteen Classic Puppet Plays *(WECAN, 2013).*

The Creation of Tone

Instruments and Tuning in Your Early Childhood Environment

SARAH WEBER

In this article, reprinted from Kindling, *Sarah offers suggestions for nurturing the children in our care through careful selection of instruments with tone that is pure and pleasing, supporting the children's incarnation. She also gives helpful advice for tuning lyres.*

Paint your room with sound. Envelop your work with tone. Nourish your children with the gift of pure, joyful, open-toned instruments, handmade with love and reverence, beautiful in every aesthetic and sensory way. Today we are blessed with a myriad of instruments to accompany our lives as we work and play in early childhood. The body and voice of your instruments should nurture the feeling life of the children you work with. As the caretaker, educator, or parent of a young child, it is up to you to enjoy the journey of instrument discovery. Woods, strings, iron, copper, bronze—exploring the array of instruments and their tonal qualities is the first step on your journey.

Once you have found an instrument you would like to work with, your next step will be to consider how your instrument will be tuned. But only you, yourself, ultimately will discover the instruments and tones waiting to ring forth for your children.

Instruments

Instruments should produce sounds that sing with joy and reverence. Their tones should be clear, warm, and open. Each tone should fill the room and nurture your children with a sense of well-being. Imagine the delicious smell of soup cooking, nourishing your children before they even sip their first spoonful. Can you feel that warm, comforting feeling? Imagine the instruments you play nourishing the children in a very similar way. The tonal quality, and hence the feeling you receive, from every instrument will be very personal. Ideally, you will have the opportunity to listen to an instrument before you acquire it. However, this is not always possible. So whether you can listen to and feel an instrument or not, do your research. How an instrument is built, the materials it is constructed out of, who made it—these are all factors that influence the voice of the instrument. With a bit of legwork and listening to your intuition, you should be able to choose an instrument, coming from far away if need be, that is right for you.

Currently there are many anthroposophically-inspired instruments available worldwide. Many of these instruments provide a rich and full, open-toned sound. When you first hear an instrument born out of a spiritual impulse, you immediately notice there is something special about its voice. The consciousness behind the creation of these instruments allows tones to come forth that truly imbue warmth and purity, lovely for early childhood.

To find the right instrument you will need to still your thoughts and listen. Then feel how you experience the tones of the instruments, with your children in mind. For early childhood you should seek instruments with middle- to high-pitched tones. Low tones generally are quite grounding. For our youngest children, some low tones could be too incarnating. For this same reason, in early childhood settings we avoid the beat in music and likewise drums and other rhythmic instruments. Repetitive rhythms and strong drumbeats draw us into our bodies. To help our children to gradually and naturally find a home in their bodies, music with a beat comes in when they are ready for it, typically after the nine-year-old transition.

The key to finding the right instrument for your little ones, and for yourself, is listening. A great way to enhance your listening and to truly enter into the world of tone created by instruments, is to build an instrument yourself. In every step of the process you feel the materials changing, speaking silently to you, and sounding. The instrument and its tone becomes an intimate part of you. True reverence reveals itself, as your instrument takes form and tone. This reverence carries over into your feeling life as the instrument becomes more than a tool, it becomes a friend. However your instrument came into your life, you are now responsible for its care and well-being. Instruments should be treated reverently and stored or put away properly. If you have an instrument which requires tuning, attention needs to be paid that the instrument is indeed in tune. You should listen to your instrument and tune it often. Then you can be confident that the tones you need are there when you wish to play them.

Tuning

From the Being of Music came tones, individual, pure and clear. Often their voices were not heard, not because they were not listened for, rather because, besides the human voice, we had no instruments to sing them clearly. Now we do. One way to begin this journey of the study of anthroposophical musical education for early childhood is to begin in the mood of the fifth with the tones named d′ – e′ – g′ – a′ – b′ – d′ – e″.

Every Waldorf early childhood environment should have a lyre or a glockenspiel tuned to these tones. These can be invaluable when learning or composing a song, and wonderful to improvise on during rest, play, and circle time. Having at least one instrument tuned to these tones is a great staple for your musical pantry. When working with a lyre, it is your responsibility to keep it in tune. To consciously experience and provide specific tones, you will need to be sure they are accurate. You will need tone bars, a glockenspiel, or another instrument to provide the tones to tune to. Eventually, as you become more familiar with the tones, you may be able to tune without the aid of another instrument.

Most instruments available will be tuned to a′ = 440 hertz. However, instruments tuned to a′ = 432 hertz are increasingly becoming available. Anthroposophical study has indicated that the tone at 432 hertz is the tone of the Sun.[1] The tone at 432 hertz vibrates more slowly than that at 440 hertz. Study and experience indicate that the sound of instruments tuned to 432 hertz is in harmony with our planetary reality. One must consider the effects of using instruments tuned to a faster vibration than the natural tonal movement of our sun.

I have noticed in children a great state of awareness, and calmness when we are using, or they are in the presence of, open-toned instruments tuned to 432 hertz. This is an idea, as are all ideas, open to further study and experimentation. Let your ear and your intuition guide you now that you know you have a choice.

Instruments in early childhood are invaluable. The right sound at the right time has the ability to comfort and relax an entire room of children and their adult helpers. As an educator, caretaker, or parent of young children, your instruments will be your assistants. Any time your voice or your body needs a rest, any time your words or your deeds do not seem to meet the situation, consider improvising on your instrument or playing a single tone or an entire song. Remember—still your thinking mind, listen and be free to play what comes naturally. During story, circle, painting, and playtime, your instruments, kept in tune, will be your magical treasures. When you invite their sound and music into your work and into your play, they will bring you gifts you never imagined. Your children will inwardly thank you, and you will thank your instruments.

Note

1. The particular qualities of the tone a′= 432 Hz (as contrasted to the concert pitch of a′= 440 Hz commonly used today) are discussed in Maria Renold's book *Intervals, Scales, Tones and the Concert Pitch C* (Forest Row, UK: Temple Lodge, 2004). Descriptions of experiments in the effects of different tunings are described in detail, and on page 81 the author states, "From the results given [in Chapter 16] it follows that a′ = 432 Hz may be considered to be the Sun-gold-tone."

Sarah Weber entered the world of Waldorf education through the early childhood environment and received her Masters degree in Waldorf Elementary Education at Sunbridge Institute. She also studied with Manfred Bleffert, learning about instrument-building and further explorations into tone, sound, composition, and improvisation. Sarah is a Waldorf music teacher and teaches privately in the field of anthroposophically-inspired music for children and adults.

Singing with Pre-school Children

MICHAEL DEASON-BARROW

This excerpt from a much longer article focuses on the preschool child, and is reprinted with kind permission from Kindling.

Children's Vocal Development

While we have progressions for children's musical and instrumental development, it is hard to find such developmental progressions regarding what we should expect in terms of children's vocal development—namely what is *natural* for their voices to do—or how to listen for the sounds of this development. Surely we should have concerns about this, given the goal of matching all aspects of children's music making to their innate development?

Fortunately, some well-known academics have researched and written up this question (including Graham Welch, Leon Thurman and Carol Klitzke). Having said this, like much research it remains hidden away behind the doors of academia and struggles to find its way into classroom practice. So here, first of all, are some insights on the growth of children's vocal anatomy—inspired by the book *Bodymind and Voice*, edited by Thurman and Welch.[1]

Laryngeal dimensions increase slowly and steadily in size and firmness throughout childhood. Likewise, the vocal folds increase their total length by about 6.5 mm between the ages of one to twelve. In the first few years of a child's life, the vocal folds are made up primarily of mucosal tissue. Only around the age of two to three years old does the thyroarytenoid muscle—the vocal folds ligament—begin to develop, which gradually gives the vocal folds more stability and structure. Consequently, only by age ten are the vocal ligament and mucosal tissues considerably developed.

In the same vein, the vocal tract—which extends from the true vocal folds to the exterior surfaces of the lips—is also very short in early childhood. Until the age of two years the tongue lies entirely in the oral cavity, and then its base begins the gradual descent into the pharynx, so that by the age of four, the posterior one-third of the tongue is located in the pharynx. Only by age five is the basic adult configuration of the vocal tract present, but of course this does not mean it has reached its full size. Only by age nine will the curved contour of the vocal tract be comparable with that of an adult, but even then it still remains shorter and smaller.

This tube (the vocal tract) has acoustic properties quite apart from the pitch and harmonics produced by the vocal folds. Sound waves that are emitted from the vocal folds pass through a series of linked containers (or resonators) and each contains its own timbre and sound quality. In fact, each different-sized resonator has different frequencies and amplifies particular overtones that are emitted from the vocal folds.

Therefore, in each phase of childhood the child's voice has a distinctive and underlying anatomy which produces specific modes of singing, because the vocal folds, the larynx, the vocal tract, the resonators and the tongue of the young child are completely different from those found in adults' singing. Clearly, this all causes a young child's sung tone to have totally different qualities from those of an adult.

As an example of this, consider how, when children sing on their own, without adults, you can hear how their voices easily lift up into higher pitches and bright open timbres. But when children sing together as a class with an adult you often hear how they push their voices—called "pressed phonation" by voice experts—which leads them to use a lower pitch range. In short, it is easy to assume that children sing in the same range as most non-specialist adult singers. Of course, when young children do not have good models to imitate you will hear how their pitch range is similar to that of an adult, namely, it is often found to be lower.

This situation is further exacerbated today by the fact that children in their early years primarily hear "popular" singers using a type of singing called "belt voice" which is based on a heavy, strong contact of the vocal folds. Such a very physical way of singing—which is fine for the energy and emotions that stand behind most "popular" forms of music and for older teenagers—is wholly inappropriate for pre-school children's vocal instruments, and the open nature of pentatonic music. In this connection it is important to recognize how the type of voice use—or timbre—needed to match the inner qualities of pentatonic music is just as significant as the pitches and rhythms of pentatonic music.

Questions for Teachers

What are the characteristic qualities of pre-school children's voices based on their anatomy? What you will hear are some of the following: a forward, light and bright resonance; higher, light-filled frequencies full of high harmonics; open vowels and a wonderful etheric ring.

What does all this mean for the practicing teacher? Firstly, we need to be aware that the teacher tends to inwardly hear and recognize only the timbre of his or her own particular voice type. Thus we need to teach ourselves to hear other textures and colors of the voice outside the parameters determined by our own experiences.

Secondly, we typically provide child-sized equipment for children and adjust tasks to their physical capabilities. Surely, therefore, this should also apply to singing? Sadly, however, this is seldom the case because teachers tend to look upon singing as a "natural" activity which requires no conscious awareness on the part of the teacher. Alas, however, teachers' voices are full of unhealthy and unconscious vocal habits, which the children imitate.

Clearly, the development of children's singing voices in their early years takes place primarily through the way they *imitate* the voice of the teacher. Thus it is crucial that teachers ask the question, *How can I provide an appropriate vocal model for the children to imitate?*

In particular, the teacher needs to develop her voice so that it can manifest:

- etheric ring, provided by the teacher's work with singing exercises inspired by the Werbeck method[2]
- forward, light, and bright resonance, caused by the vocal folds being amplified by the nose, the sinuses, and the hard palate (as opposed to the warmer, fatter, heavier resonance that adults typically use through the resonance of the pharyngeal tube). This should take place without recourse to any physical force, for when singing becomes just a physical activity the etheric tone that is natural in a child's voice is lost. Moreover, such physical voicing represents the polar opposite to the open, labile, floating quality of pentatonic music in the mood of the fifth.

In addition, the teacher needs to be able to model the following vocal qualities:

- lots of breath movement, good line and a strong sense of phrasing
- open-throatedness
- legato articulation
- clear, resonant vowels
- good use of the self (a well-balanced use of the body so that unnecessary movements such as pulling the head back or tongue retraction do not compromise the singing).

"It's the Ear which Sings"—ALFRED TOMATIS[3]

While we all easily understand that children do not fully physically mature until puberty and beyond, we rarely ask questions such as, "Does the structure of a child's ear actually change throughout the maturation process, or does the ear actually change the way it perceives because of the way the physical structure develops during maturation?"

It is clear from modern research that the younger the children are, the more they hear in higher frequency bands. This means that just as a cat or a dog responds to frequency bands that we do not hear, so children in their early years hear overtones more clearly than we do as adults. Furthermore, in this connection, research clearly points to the way that babies, toddlers, and pre-school children imitate the timbre, color or resonating properties of their teacher's voice more than they do the outer pitch. That is, the teacher's mode of voice production is more influential with regard to the children's pitch-matching skills than the actual note the teacher is singing.

Higher frequencies and overtones also play a big part in helping children focus the muscles of their middle ear. But what we find today is that the mechanisms involved in this focusing must be intact or it is difficult for children to match the pitch they are hearing with appropriate movements of the vocal folds. Thus Dr. Alfred Tomatis expressed great concern about the growing influence of electronic bass guitars—to this the author would also add the use of walkmans and iPods—because of his concern that this was going to de-tune the responsiveness of children's hearing. In addition, the tendency for adults to sing using pharyngeal resonance also leads to a tonal spectrum lacking in higher harmonics.

It is my firm belief that "attention deficit disorder" today is clearly linked to this question, because the majority of children with this disorder find it very difficult to focus/concentrate their listening and attention on one signal in an aural environment because they are being disturbed by all the noises and sounds in the whole environment around them. This phenomenon is often the result of the damage done by the media they are using to listen to music.

It is also important to become aware of how *smiling* when singing can influence hearing acuity. The risorius muscle reaches out from underneath the lips on its way to the ears and actually stimulates the hearing process because of the stretch it receives in smiling. (This crucial insight comes from the work of Alfred Tomatis.)

The Eustachian Tubes and the Larynx

Up until approximately age nine, the child's singing voice is primarily formed and influenced by the people who sing around them (parents, caregivers and teachers). What we hear from the children's voices is almost an echo of our own voice, as if we were calling into a cave and hearing the echo come back. In other words, the movements of the child's larynx are formed by the way they imitate adult models. Indeed, I have frequently found that when children imitate poor adult models you can often set up vocal habits that can block their voices for the rest of their lives. How does this happen?

The child's larynx is very flexible and receptive. Via the mediation of the eustachian tubes the larynx speaks to the ear and the ear speaks to the larynx. This inner-to-outer connection/pathway is much more open in young children's anatomy than in an adult's anatomy. It is therefore much more susceptible to the influence of our adult voices.

While in one sense you can say that the ear and the larynx are two individual organs, they also work very closely together. Thus it is important to look upon them as a unity. Because the ear and the larynx are not each enclosed within themselves like the eye, what enters through the ear influences the larynx and vice versa. Summing this up, Dr. Eugen Kolisko—who worked with Mrs.Werbeck and Rudolf Steiner on bringing etheric tone into voicework—said,

> *Through the eustachian tubes the activity of hearing is conveyed inwards, as they connect the larynx to the ear anatomically and physiologically. Through this activity . . . the eustachian tubes make the two organs—ear and larynx—into a unity. . . When we hear someone speaking and he says the word 'tree,' we speak the word 'tree,' too, with our etheric body . . . it etherically resounds in the so-called eustachian tubes.*[4]

In other words, what the child hears is inwardly accompanied sympathetically by his larynx. The other person *sings in me*, which brings with it a sense of the social and moral responsibility we bear in this realm. (This is also one of the reasons young children can learn languages so much quicker in their early years.)

With these thoughts in mind, it is now possible to explore the crucial importance of the vocal model the teacher provides for children to imitate.

Influence of the Teacher's Vocal Model on Children's Pitch

Pre-school children hear the sound and timbre of the teacher's voice—the vocal tract behavior of the singer—in the foreground of their consciousness, more strongly than the pitch the teacher wants them to imitate. This can be hard for adults to understand because we hear in a completely opposite way: we focus on the pitch, not the timbre.

Over the years I have experimented with this question many times and found a significant correlation between children's pitch accuracy and the quality of the vocal model the teacher is providing. In short, the pitch the teacher is offering can be obscured by many obstacles.

- *Vibrato* in the voice is a source of great confusion to young children because for them it is difficult to find the pitch within the wobbling tone of the vibrato.
- *Breathiness* or *free air* in the teacher's voice distorts the tone and makes it difficult for the children to hear the center of the pitch they are being asked to match.
- When a singer sings the same pitch but uses *different forms of resonance* (e.g. pharyngeal versus nasal resonance), then the pitches can sound higher and lower to a child. In addition, they can sound flatter and sharper and this has huge consequences for children's capacity to hear a pitch and immediately reproduce it. In particular, the use of *pharyngeal resonance*, which characterizes most adult voice use, leads to tones that are full of deeper harmonics, which confuses many children. (The pharynx is the resonator that rises up from the level of the vocal folds to behind the eyes and is divided in vocal anatomy into the laryngeal pharynx, the oro pharynx, and the nasal pharynx.) This means the higher harmonics typically found in children's voices are missing and this tends to confuse children so they do not agree on the pitch.
- In addition, when singing is *louder* this can change the pitch for some children.

In short, the voice use and tonal quality of a teacher's singing affects the child's pitch discrimination. Poor tone quality on the part of the person teaching a melody often causes pitch inaccuracy.

In the main, as I said above, children's voices are naturally more forward and brighter than an adult's voice, because of the different dimensions of their vocal tract and the different size of their vocal folds compared to those of an adult. What all specialists in this field would agree upon is that pre-school children have the best chance of responding successfully to a given target pitch if the vocal model provided is as close as possible to the typical bright resonance and timbre produced by these children's voices. Thus it is crucial for the teacher to learn how to sing using a bright, forward, and unpressed voice so that the sound is pinging off the resonators that lie forward and up from the vocal folds (the hard palate, the nose, and the sinuses) rather than being hidden back and down in the pharyngeal tube.

Male Teachers Singing with Children

One of the questions I am most frequently asked is connected to the question of male singers teaching songs and singing to young children because their voices sound in a different/lower octave from both women's and children's voices. Male teachers often ask, "Should I sing in my falsetto voice so that I sing the same pitch as the child?" My response would be "No," because in order to sing in falsetto the vocal folds behave in a totally different way to those of children, not least because they are under much greater tension compared to those of a young child and we don't want children imitating this form of voice use.

Consequently, the best advice I can offer for the male teacher is to sing with light, forward, bright resonance, and to play the actual start-up notes on an instrument like a lyre or harp, as you simultaneously sing. Best of all, simultaneously play the pitches of the melody on the lyre as you sing, because the lyre plays in the same octave as the children's voices sing.

The Teacher's Singing Voice

Teachers need to take the quality of their own singing voice seriously, not least because it radiates a sense of their well-being—or lack of well-being—to the children. Children also need to sense that their teacher is working on his or her own voice and how this is part of a path of self-development. In my experience, teachers working on their own voices find that it can be a source of regeneration and health in their lives.

Today, children are generally taught singing out of the idea that letting them just sing naturally is the right methodology. Of course, babies do sing correctly—so correctly, in fact, that adults should learn from them. Thus we should ask, how can one help the child not to lose this way of singing as she grows older? The answer is by providing the child with a wonderful culture of singing to imitate. But this means we must be a wonderful example to them in the first place.

Consequently, we need to be constantly vigilant concerning the health of the sound of the children's voices. We need to wake up to questions of the role teachers have regarding "voice care," because many children's voices today sound either edgy, harsh, loud and pressed; or very thin and breathy.

So what constitutes unhealthy voice use in the pre-school environment? Above all the teacher needs to guard against the following unhealthy elements in singing:

- Pressed/pushed phonation. This leads to the "closed quotient" time the vocal folds stay together being too long, which leads to fixity, a loss of movement, hardness in the voice, and a sense of closure
- The use of breathiness or free air in the voice. Many pre-school teachers deliberately add breath to their voices in a mistaken effort to make their voices lighter and more like what they perceive the children's to be
- The use of pharyngeal resonance

- High, shallow breathing
- Noisy intakes of breath, which irritate the vocal folds, draw children away from the listening space, and cause shallow breathing
- Tongue retraction
- Vowels produced without the aid of the tongue and the lips. Many teachers erroneously think vowels are created in the laryngeal throat region
- Inflexible, monochrome dynamics
- Lack of breath flow through the phrase, leading to syllabic note-by-note singing

If you hear vocal problems or sounds and do not understand why or how they are occurring, then I suggest trying to make that sound yourself as an imitative process, because this will often suggest the solution to you. Above all, consider taking voice lessons yourself!

Voices of Wonder and Awe

The sound of children's singing today can lack brilliance, resonance and clarity. It can sound either very forced or very dull and cloudy. One of the big influences on this dullness and lack of luster in some children's voices today is connected to the numbing external influences of the world upon both children's and adults' lives. These influences can cause teachers to deaden their voices gradually over the course of their lives and this chips away at their human aliveness and vitality (and the aliveness and vitality of children's voices).

In particular, the qualities of *awe* and *wonder* are lacking in the world in which we live, although Waldorf kindergartens, of course, work hard to make sure children can encounter these qualities in their early years. So it is exactly these qualities of awe and wonder that the children need to experience in music and their singing. As James Jordan says, "Awe and wonder are the only true vehicles for music making."

Thus a central question I have is: "How can we awaken a picture of the *whole human being* in singing?" This is a key question for teachers because at present you can only find physical/anatomical, emotional, and scientifically informed ways of working with the singing voice in singing teachers' studios and school classrooms.

However, during the early years of the child (by this I mean up to approximately the age of nine), it is important that we do not draw their attention strongly to their physical body in singing via exercises that are designed to work on specific elements of vocal anatomy. Nor should abstract technical exercises divorced from the context of a song be countenanced. Where the teacher feels help needs to be given to the children's voices it should be done via pictures, stories, lots of movement and gesture, vocal play, and improvisation—all of which should be connected to the songs being taught.

What is almost completely absent is a sense of working with the *spiritual* and *etheric* nature of the singing voice, a voice that manifests more than the personal subjective realm and more than the physical body.

Freeing the voice from the effects of today's civilization, which is leading to an increasing hardening of the physical body, is truly important and meaningful work for any teacher. This work would hardly be known about at all were it not for the work of Jürgen Schriefer and Valborg Werbeck-Svärdström. Out of their awareness of these questions they created exercises to strengthen the etheric stream in both children's and adults' voices.

Singing and the Etheric Body

Mrs. Werbeck's "School of Singing for Uncovering the Voice"—validated by Rudolf Steiner—gives teachers a wonderful way of learning how to bring the etheric body into their voices in such a way that it sounds freely in the "listening space." Given the importance of young children's imitative capacities, it is vital that pre-school teachers learn how to bring their etheric body into sounding, not just their physical and astral bodies. (To go into this is beyond the scope of this article. In addition, one needs to work with a Werbeck-trained singing teacher on the appropriate exercises which need both regular practice and feedback.)

In this connection, Dr. Eugen Kolisko said, "When children are allowed to sing at the top of their voices in school, they push the process of singing into the lower bodily organization. A kind of pressing together, a blockage occurs: this has a hardening influence on the ether-body. . . With the */ng/* singing [a Werbeck exercise] the child swings the sounds upwards. . . widens the inner spaces of the head and releases blockages in the body."[5]

At this point, it is important for me to say that I recognize that all singing should not be about the spirit nature of the human being. Of course, we should also have feeling-full singing, as well as embodied voices, allied to joy and fun. But I am making a plea for a deeper spiritual understanding of singing, as this is so absent in singing pedagogy. In addition, we should recognize that a young child's singing is naturally characterized by etheric and spiritual qualities, whereas adults' voices are obviously heavier and more physical as well as informed by the more subjective sphere of our feeling life.

The Mood of the Fifth and Its Implications for Singing

Reinhild Brass, in her booklet "Singen in der Schule," points out how the imitative forces of the child's voice can truly be connected to the openness and lightness of the mood of the interval of the fifth. Thus, the pentatonic mood is a wonderful aid not only to children's listening, musicality and the development of their consciousness, but it also aids their singing voices.

On the other hand, too early a use of the more inward intervals (e.g. the major and minor third, which bring with them a new consciousness of the beat and human astrality) takes the child in a more interior direction and leads to an early loss of both their imitative capacities and the light, spacious free-floating quality of their voices. In fact, you could say it removes their voices from the "listening space" of the periphery.

Thus we can speak about learning to sing with a voice that matches the qualities of pentatonic music in the mood of the fifth. In short, pentatonic music is not just about pitches and rhythms, but also about the voice quality.

Notes

1. Thurman and Welch (eds.), *Bodymind and Voice: Foundations of Voice Education* (National Center for Voice and Speech, Wendell Johnson Speech and Hearing Center, The University of Iowa, 1997).

2. This singing method was developed by Valborg Werbeck-Svärdström (1879-1972), a Swedish Opera singer, in order to heal and rehabilitate her own voice which had been strained by conventional singing. With Rudolf Steiner's help, she worked out of spiritual scientific principles to "uncover the voice" and connect it with the stream of cosmic music. Her book *Uncovering the Voice: The Cleansing Power of Song* is available in English (London: Rudolf Steiner Press, 2008). Her work has been continued under the leadership of Jürgen Schriefer (now retired) and Christiaan Boele.

3. The French physician Alfred Tomatis (1920-2001) was an internationally-known ear, nose, and throat specialist who developed an alternative medicine theory of hearing and listening known as the Tomatis method. He believed that listening and communication problems are at the root of many disorders, including autism, schizophrenia and depression as well as learning disorders and dyslexia. His books include *The Conscious Ear* (Barrytown, NY: Station Hill Press, 1991). For information on working with the sound */ng/* as a healing remedy for the voice, see Valborg Werbeck-Svärdström, *Uncovering the Voice*, pages 76-81.

4. Eugen Kolisko (1893-1939) was an Austrian-German physician and educator who was invited by Rudolf Steiner to work at the first Waldorf School in Stuttgart in 1920. Quotation from *Uncovering the Voice, Social Therapeutic Medical Singing Course*, private print for members of the School of Uncovering the Voice only.

5. See note 4.

Michael Deason-Barrow is director of Tonalis: Centre for the Development of Music. He has lectured in universities, been head of music in a London comprehensive school, taught in Steiner schools, and today offers courses all over the world connected to a new vision of music education.

Appendix

Learning to Hear the Mood of the Fifth

We offer the following three versions of the song "Morning is Come" to help you *hear* the differences among tunes in a major key, in the pentatonic mood, and in the mood of the fifth.

Here is the traditional version of the song, written in the key of G major (the f-sharp would not normally be notated again in the first measure, but is included here to emphasize its importance in forming the major key):

This melody is based on a G-major scale, with the g′ functioning as the "tonic" note, the note which we hear as the final resting place or "home:"

Here is a pentatonic version of the song:

This melody is based on a pentatonic (five-tone) scale. You will notice it lacks the f-sharp and the c of the G-major scale.

Here is the song in the mood of the fifth:

This version is based not on a scale, but rather on balanced movement around the central note a′.

Listening to these three melodies can illustrate some of the characteristic qualities of music in the mood of the fifth, for example:

- A mood-of-the-fifth song is balanced around a central note a′ rather than leading the ear to a final, grounded resting note.
- A mood-of-the-fifth song is not contained within the octave d′ to d″ like a pentatonic song; rather, it contains two fifths, so it extends all the way from the lower d′ to the upper e″.
- While a mood-of-the-fifth song uses the same notes as the pentatonic scale above, the notes are arranged differently, resulting in a more open, free-floating sound and feeling.

As a final example, here is the song "Let Us Form a Ring," reprinted from the collection of the same name. In this song, it is easy to hear how the melody moves around the central a′, bringing a sense of balanced lightness:

A very helpful path into mood-of-the-fifth music is Julius Knierim's seminal book, *Quintenlieder: Music for Young Children in the Mood of the Fifth* (see Recommended Resources for detailed information). Dr. Knierim describes this book as an "introduction to the mood of the fifth for adults who wish to sing, play and dance with children before their ninth year." With a minimum of words and theoretical explanation, he offers simple exercises to accustom our ear and our voice to this kind of music. Often the words of the songs are humorous, reminding us that music is meant to bring warmth and joy into our lives!

Recommended Resources

LECTURES BY RUDOLF STEINER

Steiner, Rudolf. *The Child's Changing Consciousness as the Basis of Pedagogical Practice* (Great Barrington, MA: Anthroposophic Press, 1996). See especially Lecture 3.

Steiner, Rudolf. *The Education of the Child and Early Lectures on Education* (Great Barrington, MA: Anthroposophic Press, 1996). See especially "Education in the Light of Spiritual Science" for a basic understanding of the nature of the young child and the essential qualities of an education that will benefit not only the physical but also the etheric body; and "Education and Spiritual Science" for a description of dream consciousness (page 66).

Steiner, Rudolf. *The Essentials of Education* (London: Rudolf Steiner Press, 1982). See especially Lecture 2.

Steiner, Rudolf. *The Inner Nature of Music and the Experience of Tone* (Spring Valley, NY: The Anthroposophic Press, 1983). See especially Lectures V, VI, and VII.

SONGS IN THE MOOD OF THE FIFTH

Knierim, Julius. *Quintenlieder: Music for Young Children in the Mood of the Fifth* (Fair Oaks, CA: Rudolf Steiner College Press, 1994). Rhymes from all over Europe set to new tunes in the mood of the fifth, along with guidance in how to listen for and compose in this mood.

Lonsky, Karen. *A Day Full of Song: Work Songs From a Waldorf Kindergarten* (Spring Valley, NY: WECAN, 2009). 42 original songs in the mood of the fifth, illustrated by Victoria Sander. A companion CD is also available as an aid to learning the songs.

Seidenberg, Channa. *I Love To Be Me: Songs in the Mood of the Fifth* (Stourbridge, UK: Wynstones Press). 32 songs with illustrations by Kingsley Lou Little.

Ellersiek, Wilma. *Giving Love—Bringing Joy* (Spring Valley, NY: WECAN, 2003), *Gesture Games for Spring and Summer* (WECAN, 2005), *Gesture Games for Autumn and Winter* (WECAN, 2007), and *Dancing Hand, Trotting Pony* (WECAN, 2010). In this series of songs and gesture games for children in kindergarten and the lower grades, all of the tunes are in the mood of the fifth. Two learning CDs are available: *Giving Love—Bringing Joy* and *Gesture Games for Spring, Summer, Autumn and Winter*. A selection of some of the songs and games in Spanish is also available: *Juegos de Gestos de Mano* (Editorial El Liceo, Spain / WECAN, 2012).

Foster, Nancy. *Let Us Form a Ring: An Acorn Hill Anthology of Songs, Verses, and Stories for Children* (Silver Spring, MD: Acorn Hill Waldorf Kindergarten and Nursery, 1989) and *Dancing As We Sing: Seasonal Circle Plays and Traditional Singing Games for Young Children* (Acorn Hill Waldorf Kindergarten and Nursery, 1999). Many mood-of-the-fifth songs and circles are included in these two anthologies, along with other pentatonic and traditional songs. Learning CDs are available, and both books and CDs are distributed by WECAN.

Wynstones Press. *Spring*, *Summer*, *Autumn*, *Winter*, *Gateways*, and *Spindrift* (all Stourbridge, UK: Wynstones Press, 1999). The third edition of this long-time favorite series of poems, songs, and stories for young children has been thoroughly revised to emphasize mood-of-the-fifth and pentatonic songs.

FURTHER READING

Husemann, Armin. *The Harmony of the Human Body* (Edinburgh, UK: Floris Books, 2003)

Renold, Maria. *Intervals, Scales, Tones and the Concert Pitch c=128 Hz* (Forest Row, UK: Temple Lodge Publishing, 2004)

Ruland, Heiner. *Expanding Tonal Awareness* (London: Rudolf Steiner Press, 1992).

Made in the USA
Las Vegas, NV
11 June 2024

90983853R00103